Naum Medovoy

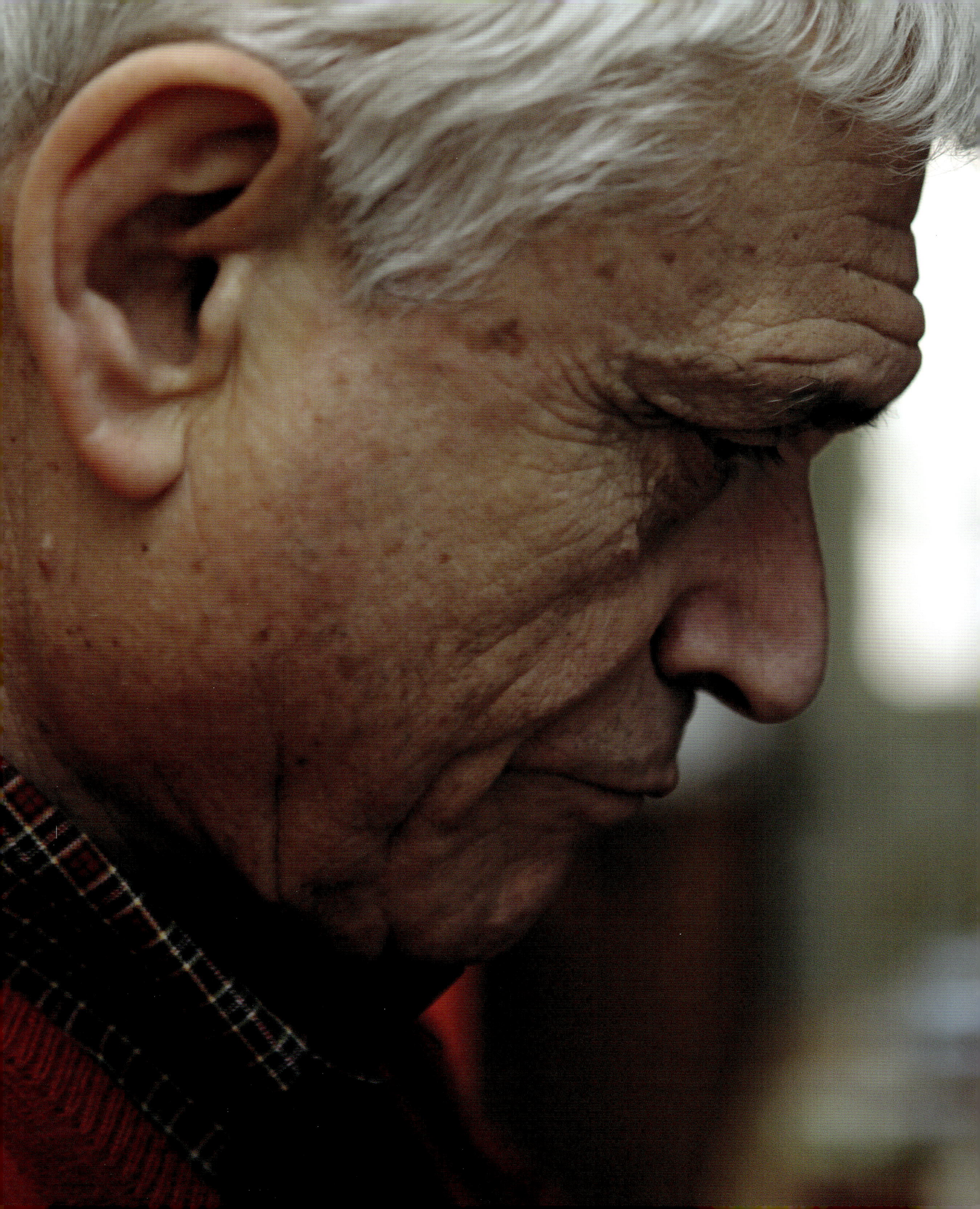

Naum Medovoy

Last March

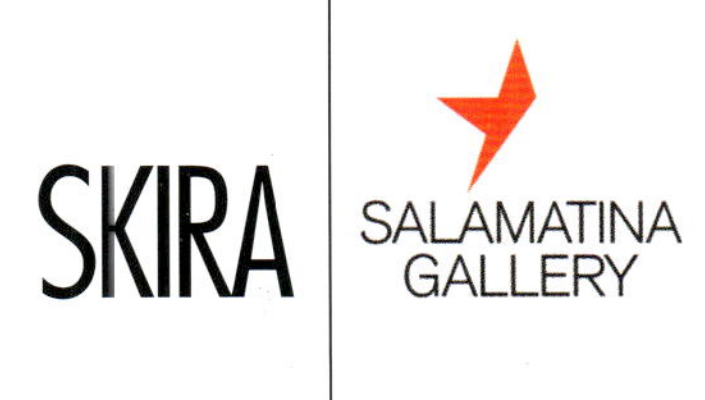

Cover
Last March 39, 2007 (detail)
Digital print, oil sticks on paper

p. 4
Naum Medovoy in his studio
in Orient, NY 2013
photo © Vladimir Semenihin

Art Director
Marcello Francone

Editor
Paola Gribaudo

Design
Luigi Fiore

Editorial Coordination
Vincenza Russo

Editing
Valeria Perenze

Layout
Sabina Brucoli

Translations
Julia Trubikhina, Oksana Salamatina

First published in Italy in 2014
by Skira Editore S.p.A.
Palazzo Casati Stampa
via Torino 61
20123 Milano
Italy

Printed and bound in Italy.
First edition

ISBN: 978-88-572-2631-6

Distributed in USA, Canada, Central &
South America by Rizzoli International
Publications, Inc., 300 Park Avenue
South, New York, NY 10010, USA.
Distributed elsewhere in the world
by Thames and Hudson Ltd.,
181A High Holborn, London WC1V
7QX, United Kingdom.

Acknowledgments

Working on Last March *is challenging. The drawings embody a narrative of the artist and his deeply felt experience—a personal expression and a reflection of what he wants the audience to feel and to relive with him. The creation of this book has been an amazing journey and collaboration between Medovoy and the authors. I am very proud that this publication is the first of its kind for this artist. Special thanks go to Trevor Tweeten, Paola Gribaudo, Amanda Glesmann, Rahim Azimov and John Cauman, the book's primary essayist. I am also grateful for the thoughtful and illuminating texts contributed by Vitaly Komar, Andrea Traubner, Trevor Tweeten and John Cauman. Daniel Neumann and Max Yawney contributed greatly to the project by providing crucial help with photography.*

Oksana Salamatina

When the very existence of civilization was challenged by Hitler in the middle of the last century,
the alliance of the two great nations, America and Russia, brought about the defeat of Hitler
and the Nazis.
John F. Kennedy, in his speech at American University, in 1963 said: "No nation in the history
of battle ever suffered more than the Soviet Union in the Second World War."
Twenty million Russian soldiers brought down the gates of Auschwitz and Buchenwald.
It is our deep belief that peace in today's world greatly depends on the friendship between
America and Russia, between Russians and Americans. This is our wish. This is our dream.

Naum Medovoy and Oksana Salamatina

Contents

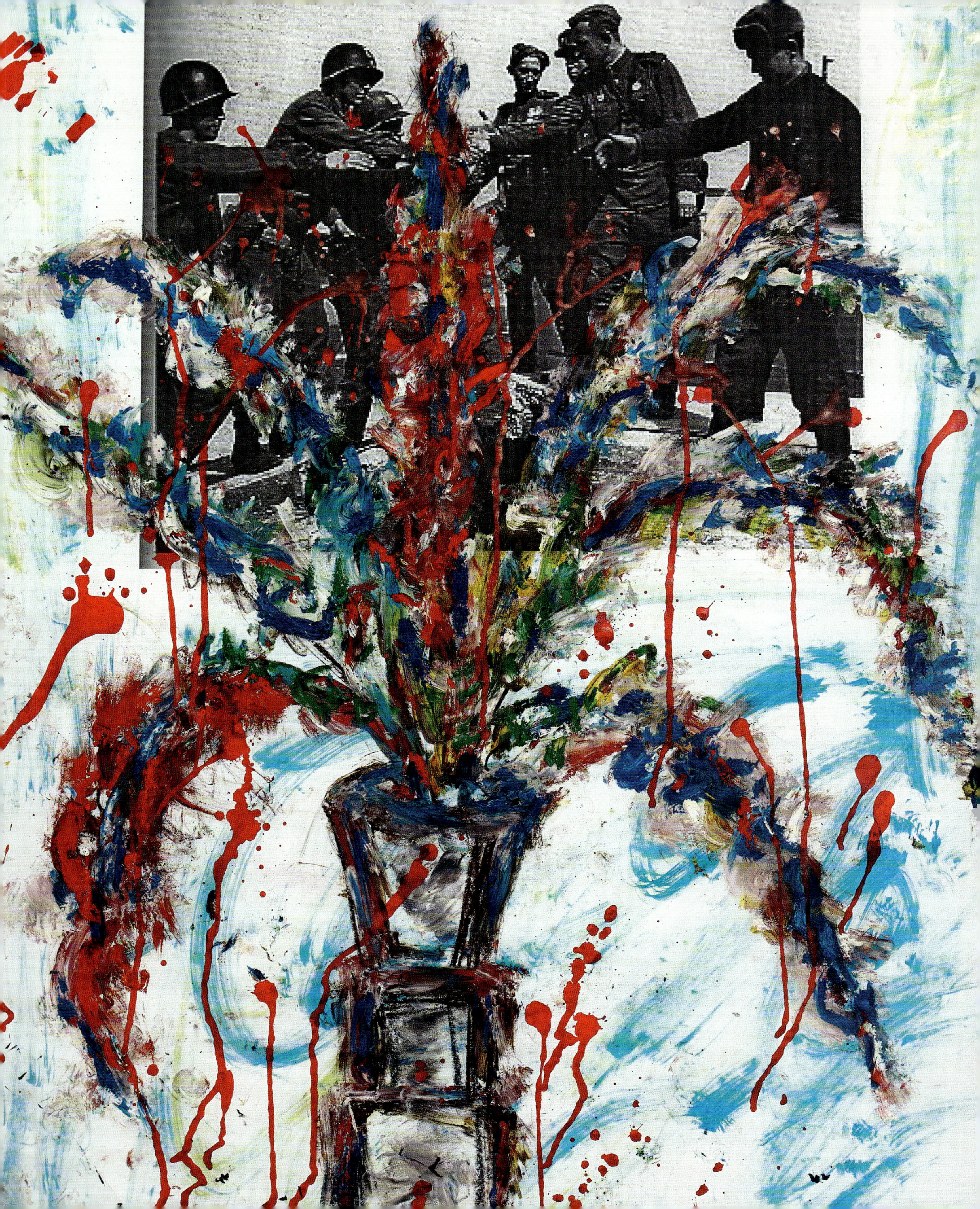

Foreword

Naum Medovoy

Most families in the Soviet Union endured great suffering during the Great Patriotic War, as World War II is known among Russians. Living in Odessa, Ukraine—part of the country at the time—my family was no exception; my grandfather, two of my aunts, and their entire families died in the Holocaust, while two of my mother's younger brothers fought in the war. One was killed in Romania, and the other, who was listed as missing in action, was never heard from again.

My father was drafted right after the war started, in June 1941, leaving four of us behind: me, my mother, my older sister, who was eight years old, and my younger sister, who wasn't even one. As the front was rapidly approaching our town, my mother feared we'd end up under German occupation. To avoid this fate, she walked us eastward alongside the retreating Russian troops. I still vividly remember that summer: the long, hot days; crowded back roads; bombings, burning fields, and makeshift refugee camps in the open air. My sister didn't survive the journey, as she fell ill and died en route.

The war finally ended on May 9, 1945, after four long years. While I was only eight years old at the time, the Day of Victory—as the Russians call it—is still one of the most important days of my life. Indeed, the Great Patriotic War and its victorious outcome lent intellectual and cultural purpose to several generations of Soviets. This holds especially true not only for me, but for filmmaker Grigory Chukhray as well, a war veteran and one of the most celebrated directors in Russia. He's perhaps most known for *Ballad of a Soldier* (1960), which received a special jury prize at the Cannes Film Festival. Later that year it broke Cold War barriers, premiering in the United States at the San Francisco International Film Festival.

Chukhray had a profound influence on my work. After graduating from film school I assisted him with *Stalingrad*. A full-length documentary on the Battle of Stalingrad—which Chukhray fought in—the film was produced by Mosfilm Studio and was especially meaningful to me since my father had also fought there. Since the film was based on original photographs and documentary footage—both Soviet and foreign—my job was to review these visuals and, in line with the director's instructions, select the most relevant ones.

Thanks to Chukhray's prominence, I was afforded access to premier Soviet cinematic and photographic archives. While the work itself was exciting, it also lent me newfound appreciation for documentary photographs, which can have a profound impact on cinematography.

When I began working on my own documentary films, archival photos became everyday working materials. This was the case with my 1972 collaboration with James Khlevner and scriptwriter Lev Arkadyev, *The Missing (The Last March)*. It was a short film that touched on the taboo topic of Russian servicemen declared "missing in action."

There were millions of these so-called "missing in action" soldiers after the war, most of whom weren't missing at all, but rather, relegated to hard labor at Gulag work camps. This perverse situation was due to Soviet army surrender codes stemming from Stalin's belief that Russian soldiers should fight and die rather than surrender. Those who do not die, he reasoned, ceased to exist. This led to soldiers captured and imprisoned by the Nazis being declared committers of treason. Thus Russian POWs were written off and declared forever missing, their families told by the authorities that they had no information on their son, husband, father, etc. He was missing, period.

In reality, almost all the men were prisoners of war, encircled and captured by Germans in the hundreds of thousands and sent to Nazi concentration camps. Those who survived the brutality of captivity were almost immediately considered criminals.

It's hard to imagine a fate more bitter than theirs. Perhaps in all wartime history, no government has treated its own soldiers with such profound injustice. *The Missing (The Last March)* is dedicated to those men and women, and was created to honor their memory.

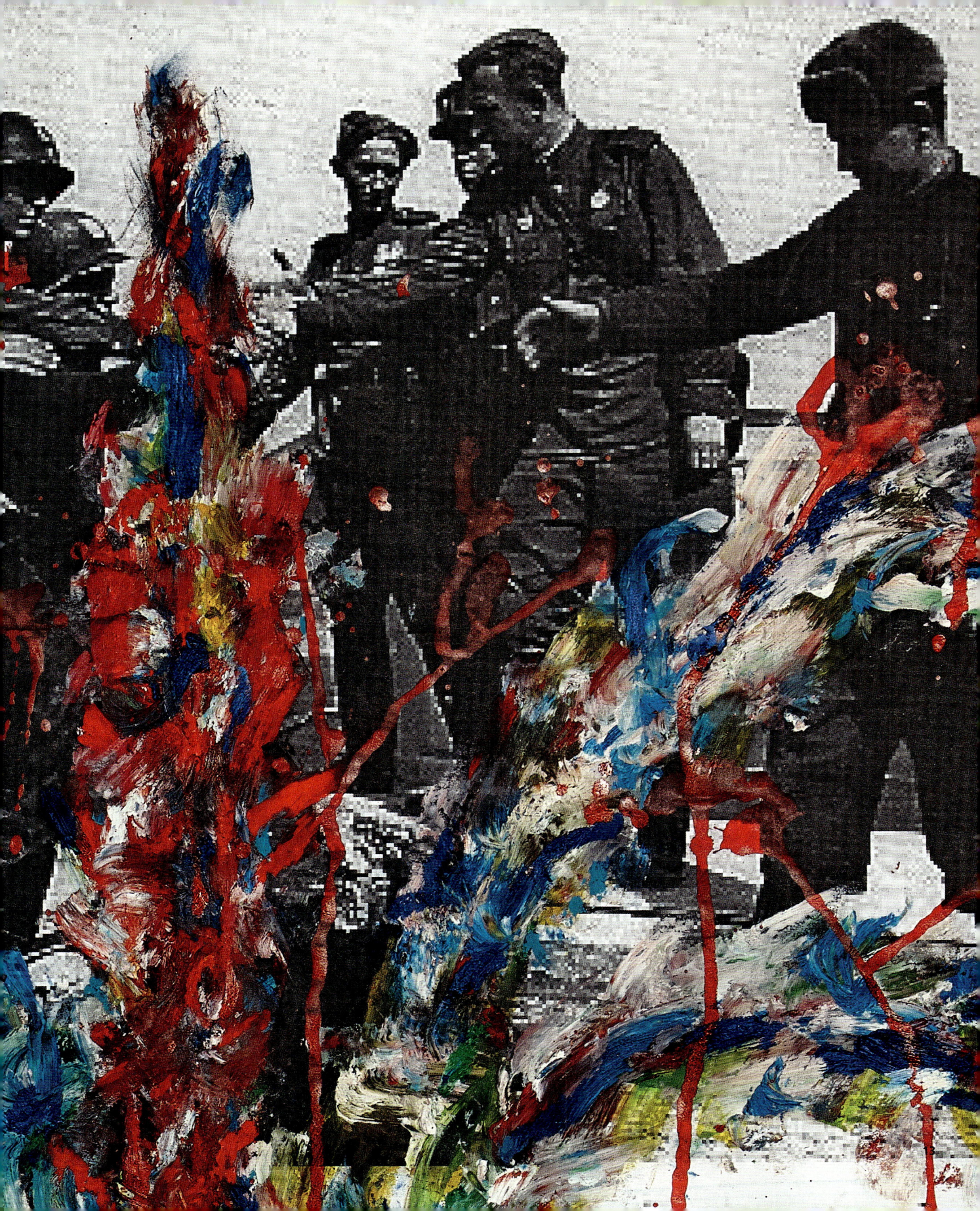

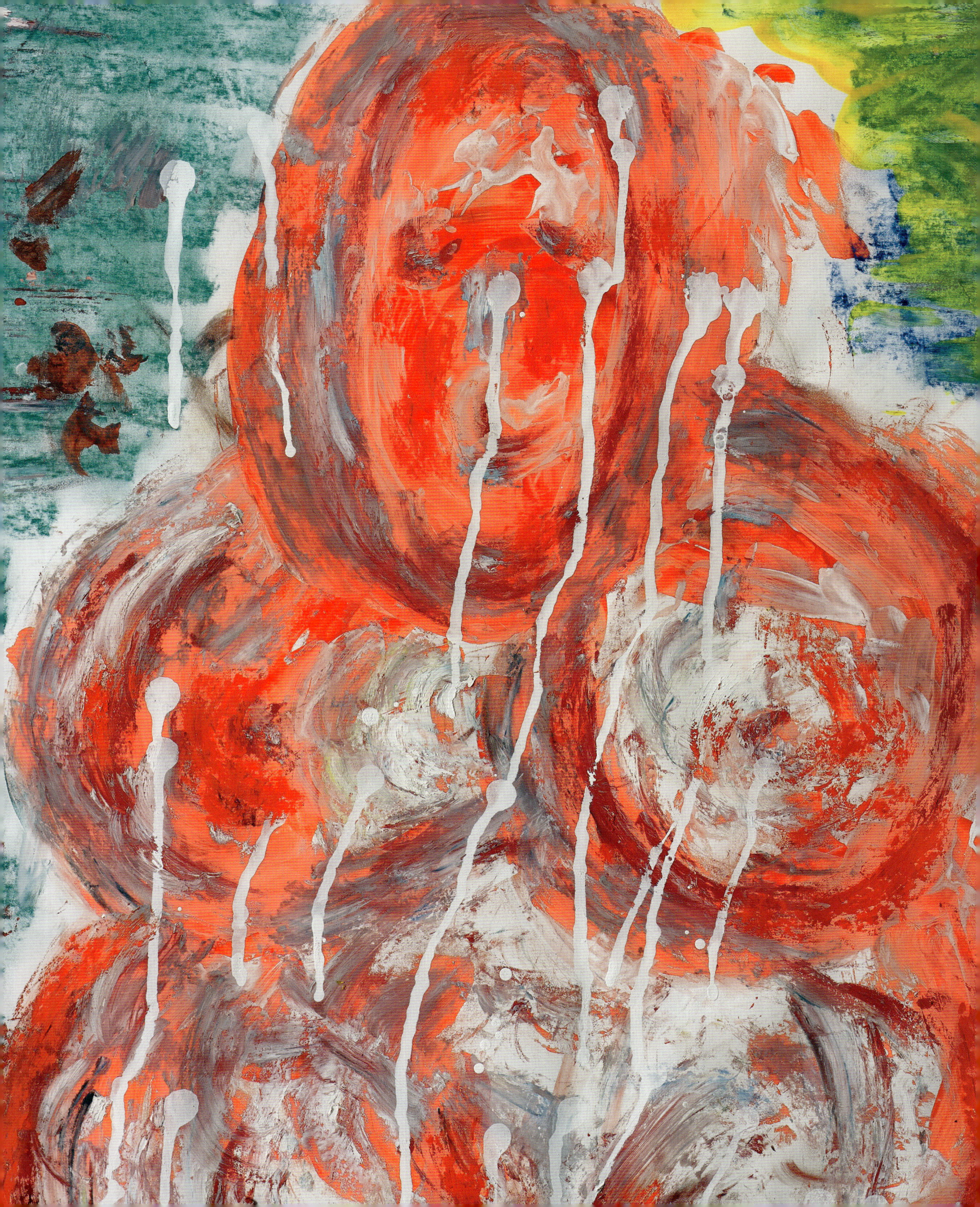

The Missing (The Last March)

Trevor Tweeten

When I first saw Naum Medovoy's documentary *The Missing (The Last March)* I was struck by its incredible cinematic imagery. It is an iconic portrait of Russia in the aftermath of World War II, a moment in history that is inadequately understood, particularly in America. In speaking to Naum I was moved by how his own life experiences are bound to the greater narrative his film and drawings explore. I was therefore interested in the potential of a video installation that could explore and reveal the layers and complexities contained both in the narrative of the original film and in this personal history. Inserting Naum into the frame was a performative gesture that created a compelling and engaging dialogue with the original film, as well as with the drawings. The imagery and the faces of the film are compassionate and deeply human, a reflection of Medovoy himself. It was a pleasure to collaborate.

Last March 1, 2007
Oil sticks and white ink on paper

pp. 16–17
Last March 1, 2007 (detail)

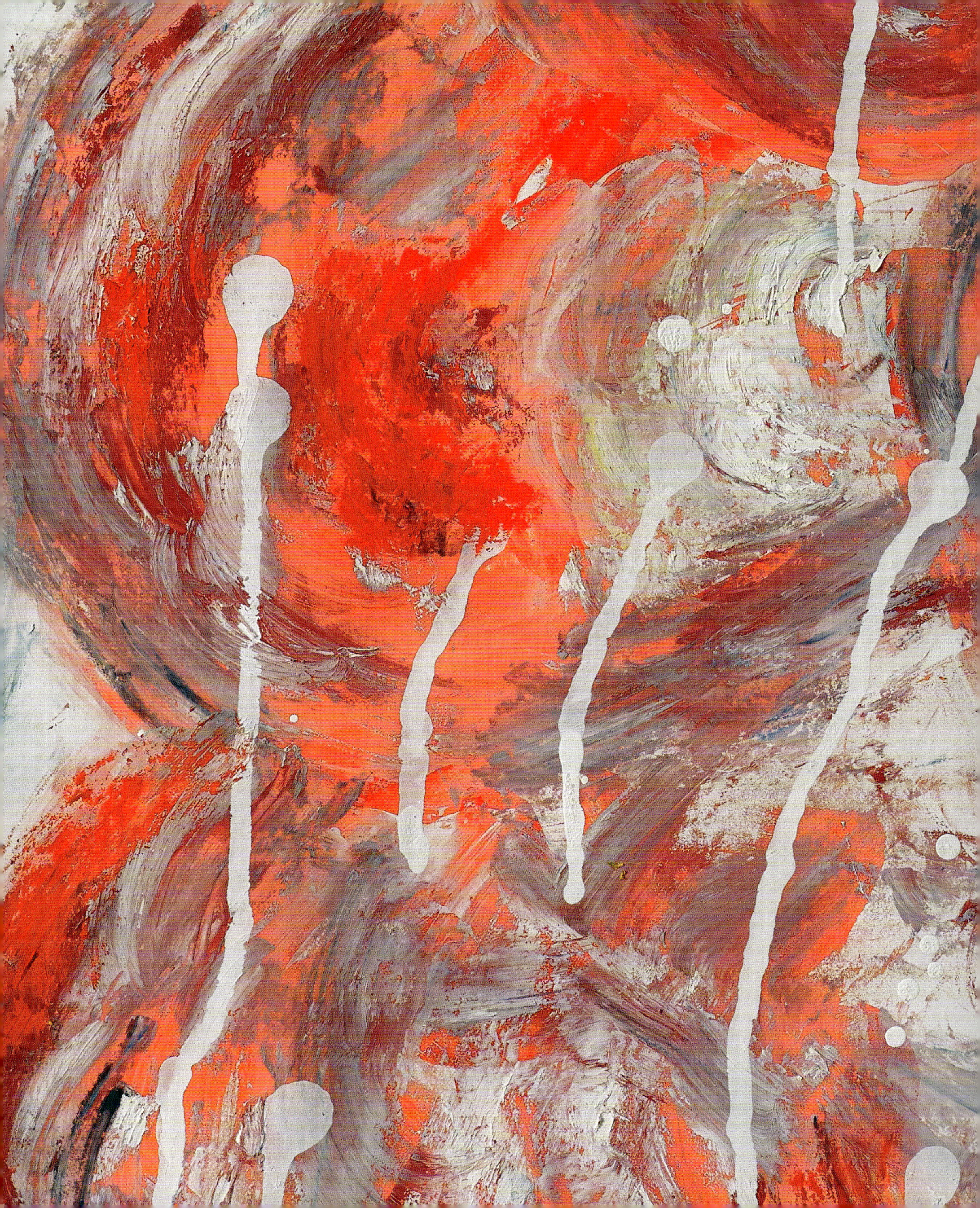

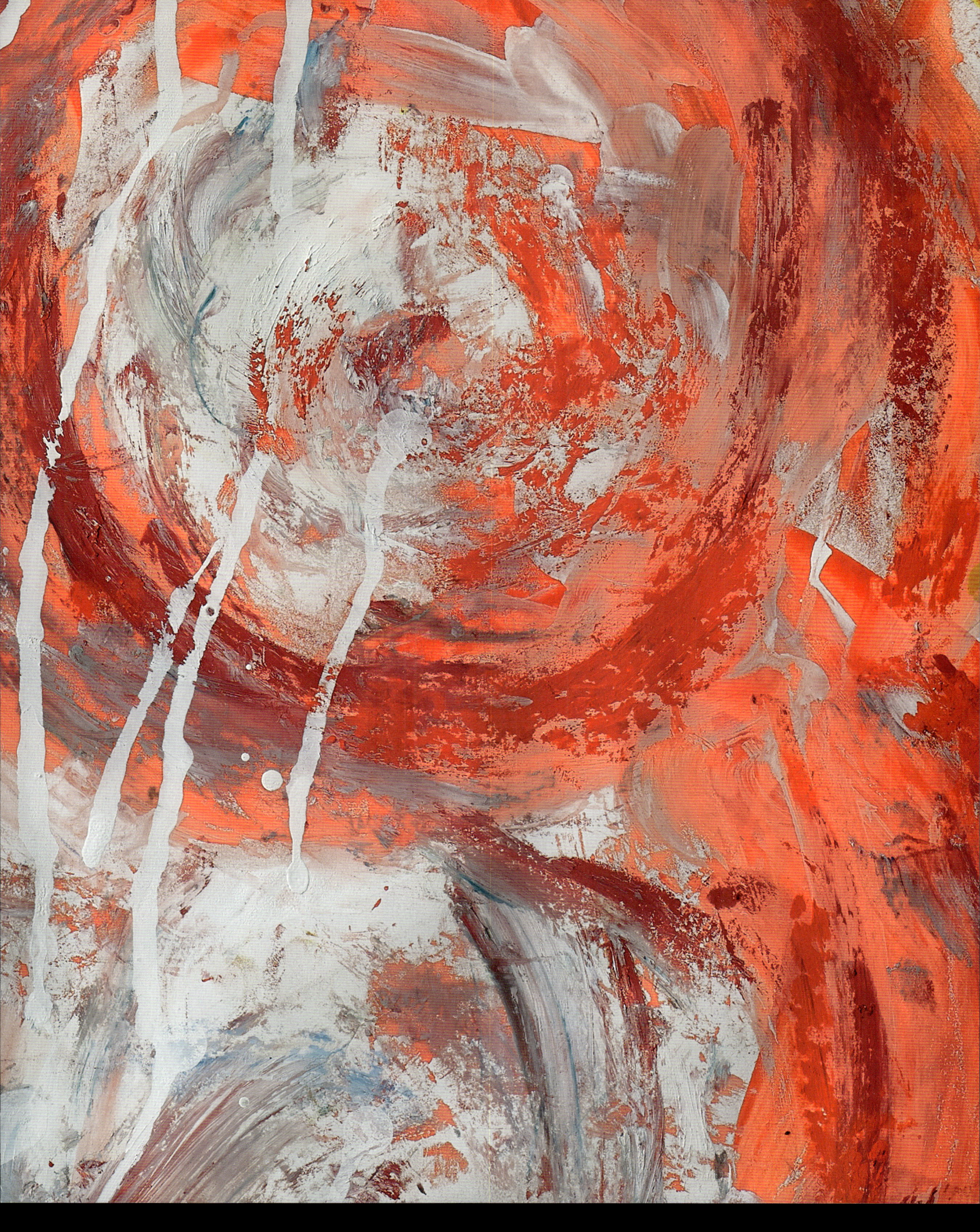

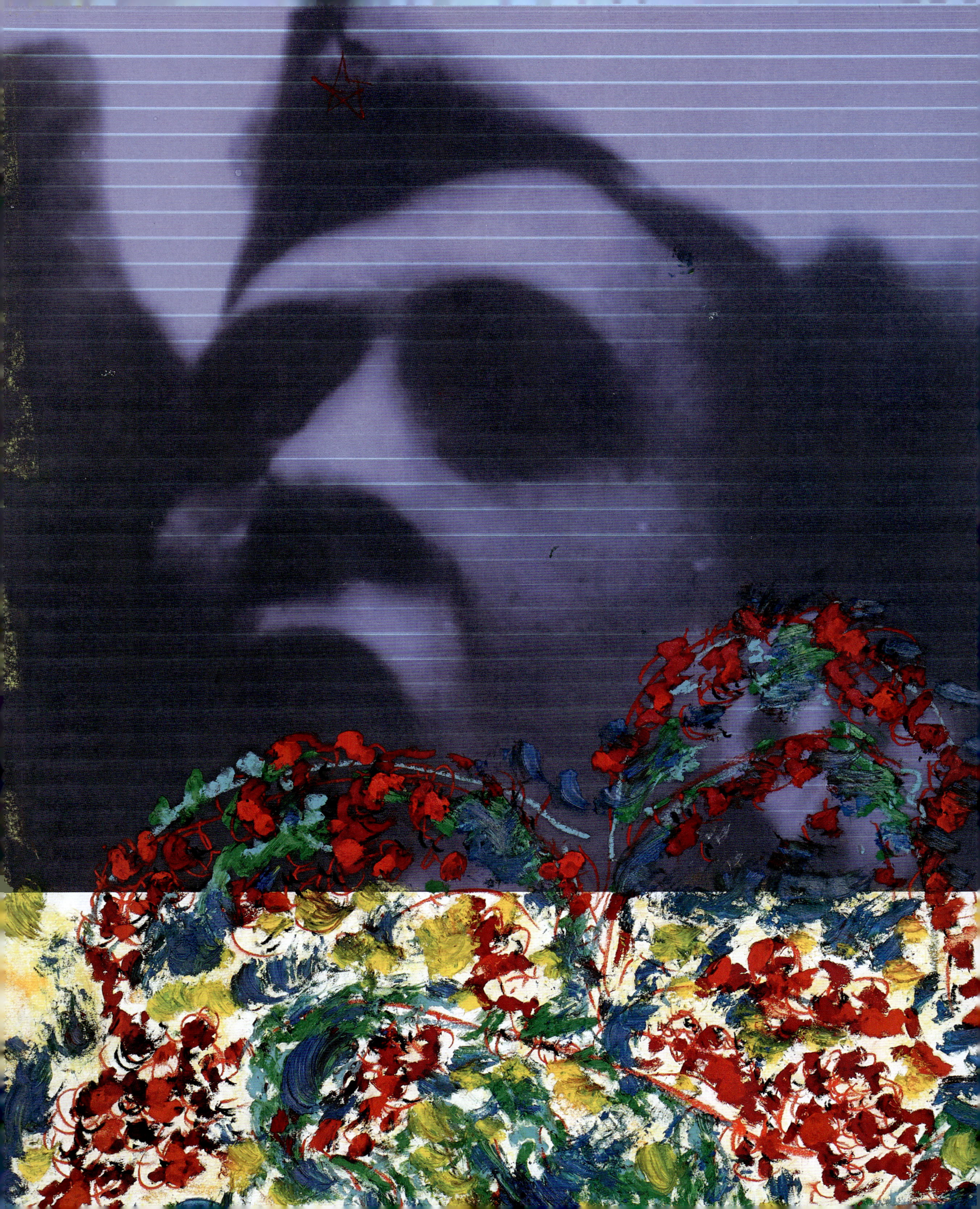

Naum Medovoy: Linescapes

Vitaly Komar

I first encountered the brilliant works of Naum Medovoy only a few years ago. A wonderful cinematographer and painter, this artist combines paradoxical trends of contemporary art. In his hands, fragments of documentary video art and black-and-white photographs from World War II enter into a moving dialogue with the colorful "explosions" of his bouquets of expressionism. This tragic dialectic reflects the contradictions of post-modern and post-Soviet consciousness and forges a "new aesthetic synthesis," closely connected to the unique lived experience of the artist. It seems to me that in Medovoy's work "objective conceptualism" cannot be separated from "subjective emotion." Within his art, visual historical images fuse with autobiographical memories of his childhood and the deeply personal emotions of a wise and experienced man and artist.

Last March 39, 2007 (detail)
Digital print, oil sticks on paper

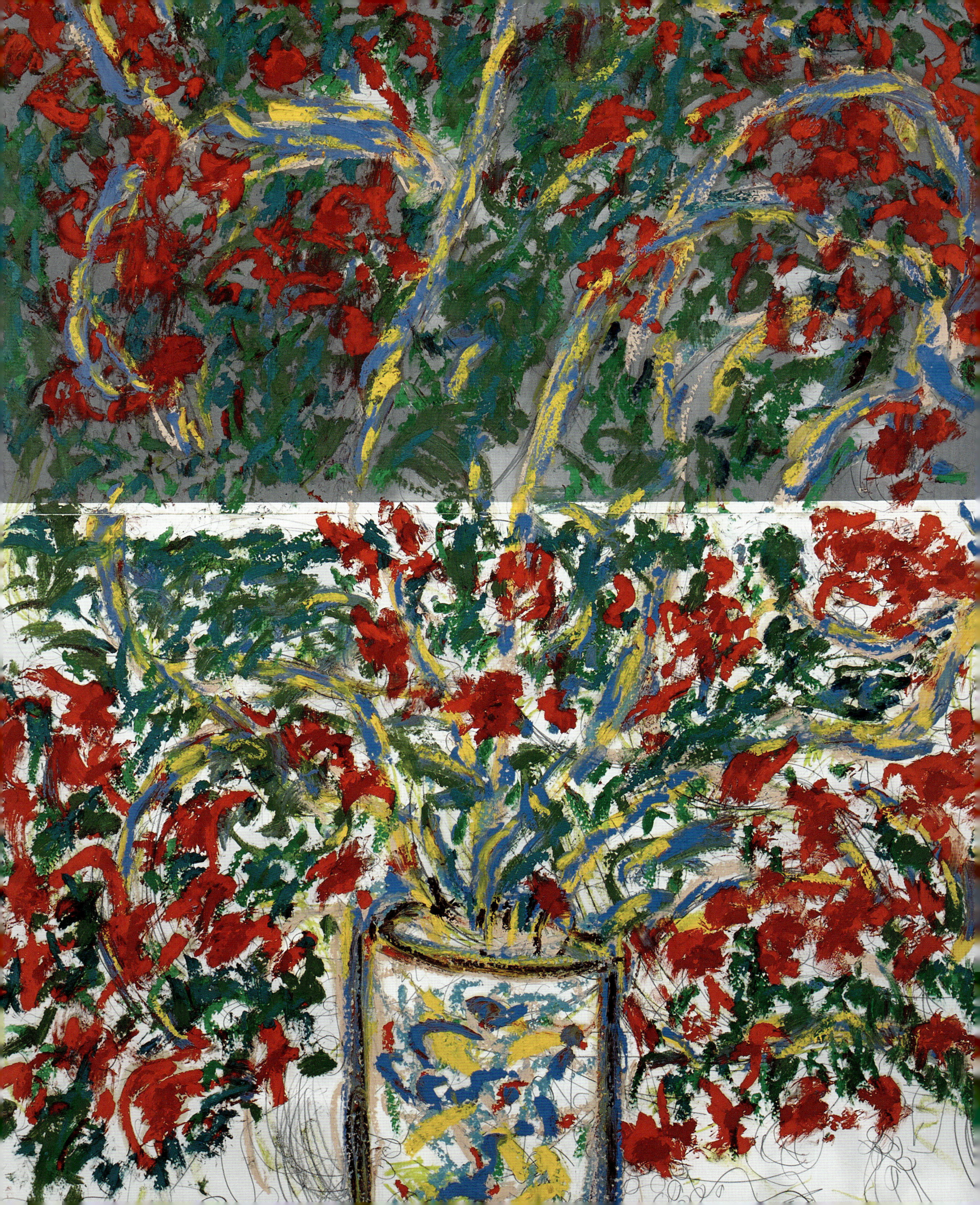

The Missing: the Film and the Paintings by Naum Medovoy

Andrea Traubner

The Missing (The Last March) was broadcast in 1985 by Thirteen/WNET, the flagship PBS station in New York, as part of its acclaimed local series about World War II: *Years of Darkness*. The film speaks with a rare poignancy about millions of Russian soldiers who fell into the category "missing." Many of them were captured by the Germans and suffered in Nazi concentration camps; a great number of them died. Thirty years after this broadcast, co-producer Naum Medovoy has revisited and drawn inspiration from the project. He has created large drawings using images from the film as his starting-point. Medovoy hopes that the film's subject will reverberate today—and encourage both Russians and Americans to find common ground for peace and brotherhood between their countries.

Last March 26, 2007 (detail)
Digital print, oil sticks on paper

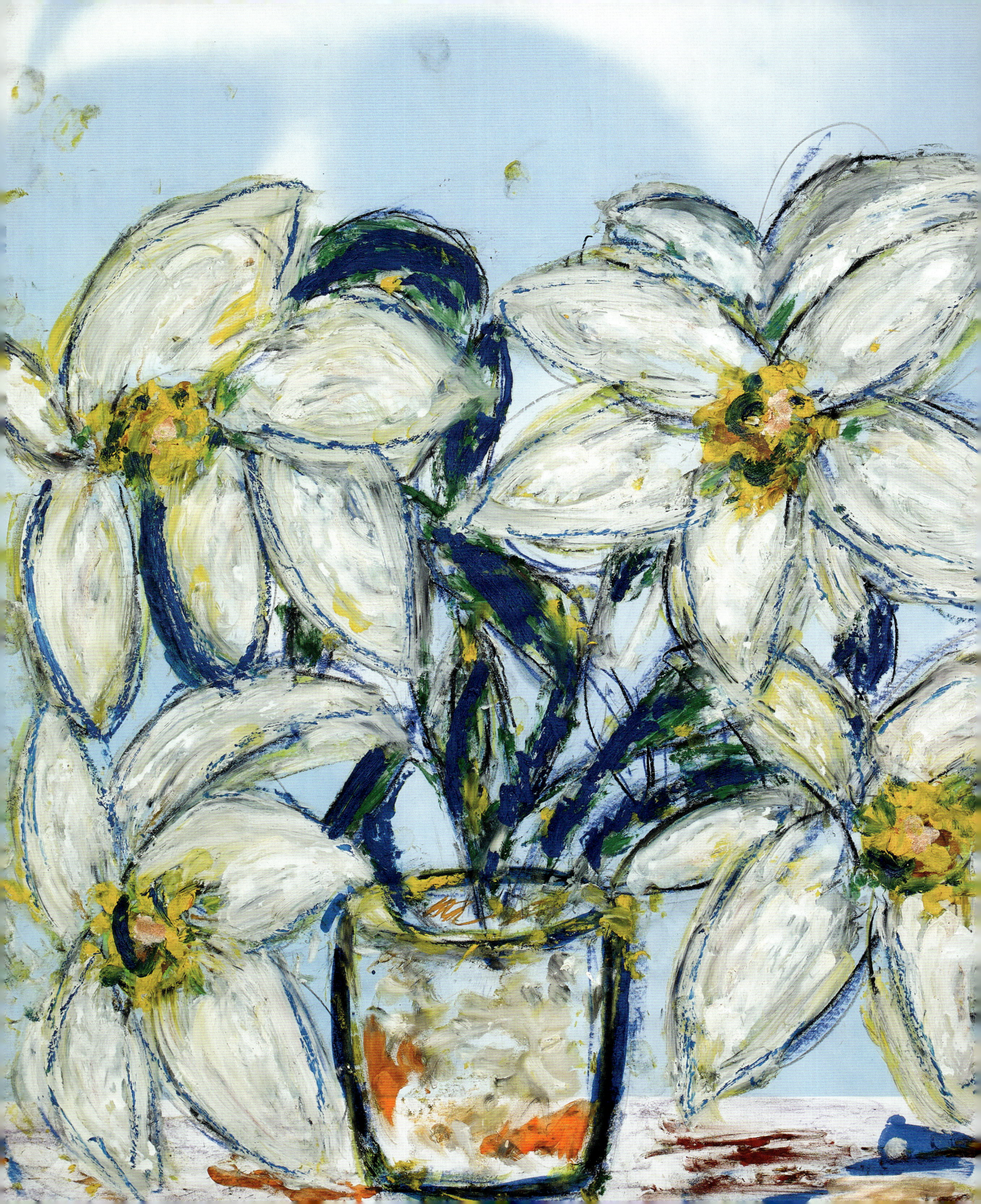

On Naum Medovoy and His Art

Oksana Salamatina

"I don't believe films change anyone's mind,
but I was spawned during the Roosevelt era, a time of great change,
and I still believe in trying to get people to think."
(Stanley Kramer, 1913–2001)

"Beauty of every description finds its charm in variety.
Nature abhors both vacuum and regularity. For the same reason,
no work of art can really be called such
if it has not been created by an artist who believes in irregularity
and rejects any set form. Regularity, order,
desire for perfection (which is always a false perfection)
destroy art."[1]

Naum Medovoy's career spans four decades. A self-taught artist, he was mostly
a documentary filmmaker until he began printing stills from his films, applying oil
sticks and black and white ink to their surfaces. The resulting works serve as platforms
for expressive and perceptual experimentation, which are often self-referential
in nature; Medovoy's photo-documentary collage paintings are rooted in his childhood
memories and previous work.
In his studio, Medovoy tirelessly works on each painting, moving between various
combinations of media until he's satisfied with the end result. In the process, he offers
an entirely new perceptual experience, such so that he's established himself as
a unique, vanguard talent in the art world, inventing new ways to aesthetically engage
viewers, mediating between oil sticks, ink, film, photography, and memory.
I came across him by chance. Our mutual friend, Vitaly Komar, saw a few exhibitions
I curated at my gallery and thought I should see Medovoy's most recent series, *Last
March* (2007). It shares the same title as his documentary film from 1972, which is
dedicated to the Soviet soldiers who didn't return from World War II. Many were
deemed traitors for their capture by the Nazis, and were sent to Soviet work camps
and never heard from again. Some simply went missing.

Last March 38, 2007 (detail)
Digital print, oil sticks on paper

For the series, Medovoy draws very frenetic, gestural marks of flowers directly onto *The Last March* film stills, which have been printed on paper. The blooms symbolize life, memory, fragility, sorrow and hope. As Elia Kazan once said, "the key word in art—it's an ugly word, but it's a necessary word—is power, your own power. Power to say, 'I'm going to bend you to my will.' However you disguise it, you're gripping someone's throat. You're saying, 'My dear, this is the way it's going to be.'"[2]

Bending us to his will, so to speak, the artist draws the viewer in. Powerfully affecting, his work leaves the viewer haunted. Monumental yet fragile, post-modern yet ultra contemporary, Medovoy's paintings have a raw and irregular beauty about them, something akin to how Baudelaire wrote "that which is not slightly distorted lacks sensible appeal; from which it follows that irregularity, that is to say, the unexpected, surprise and astonishment, are an essential part and characteristic of beauty."[3]

It is this strange appeal of Medovoy's work—which straddles the line between beauty and grotesqueness—that gives it its lasting influence and afterlife, that "grips" our throat; or as George Stevens once declared in talking about film, that bounces off the page and into the viewer's mind, like something alive and changing. The same thing can be said about Modovoy's art; it lasts with you long after you've left it.

[1] A. Renoir, in L. Venturi, *Les Archives de l'Impressionnisme*, Durand-Ruel éditeurs, Paris-New York 1939, I, pp. 127–129; see also S. Eisenstein, *Film Form: Essays in Film Theory*, Harcourt Brace, San Diego CA 1949, p. 51.
[2] E. Kazan, in G. Stevens, Jr., *Conversation with the Great Moviemakers of Hollywood's Golden Age at the American Film Institute*, Knopf Doubleday Publishing Group, New York 2009.
[3] Ch. Baudelaire, *Fusées*, 13 May 1856; see also Eisenstein, op. cit.

Last March 38, 2007 (detail)

pp. 26–27
Last March 2 (Two. Not together), 2006 (detail)
Oil sticks on paper

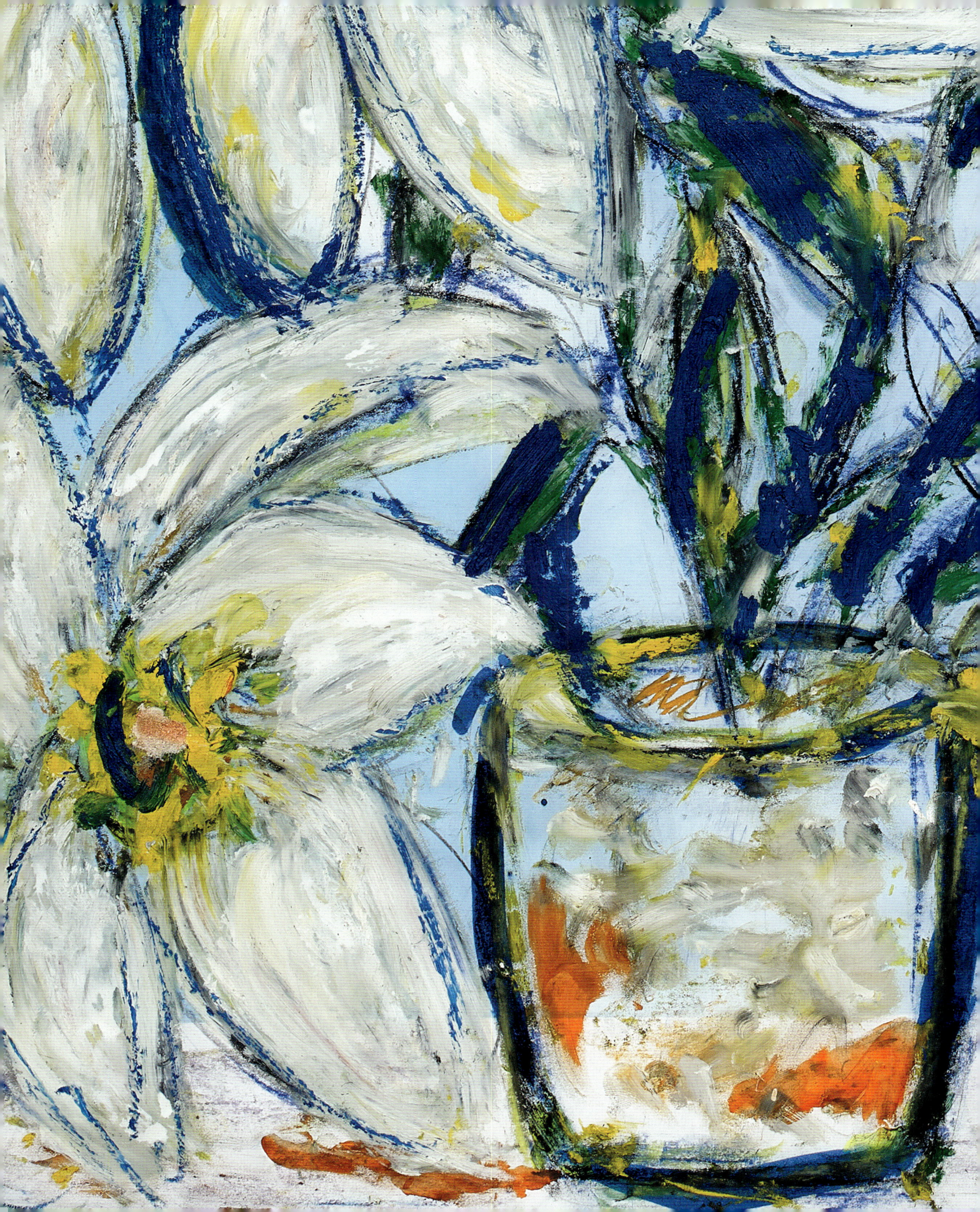

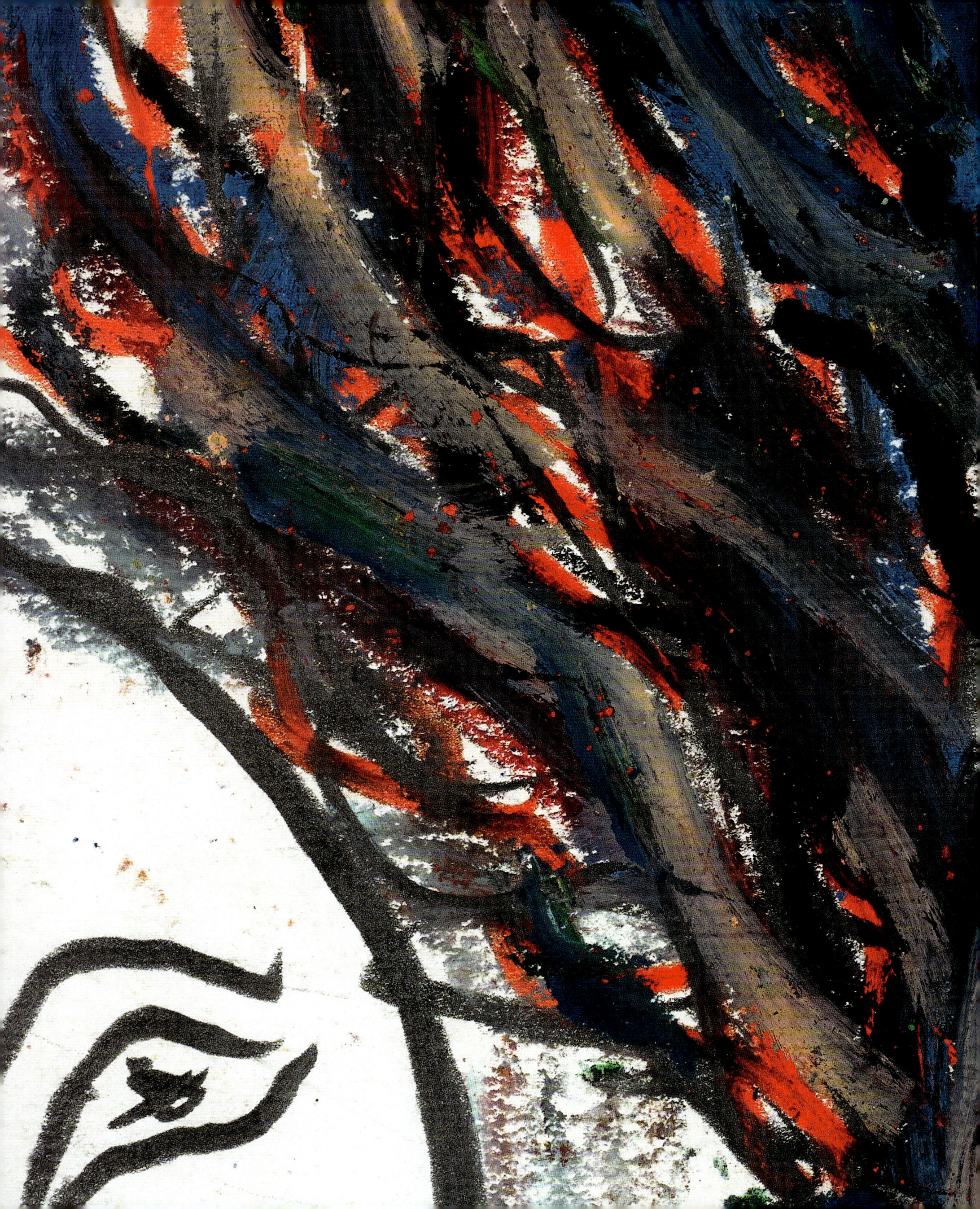

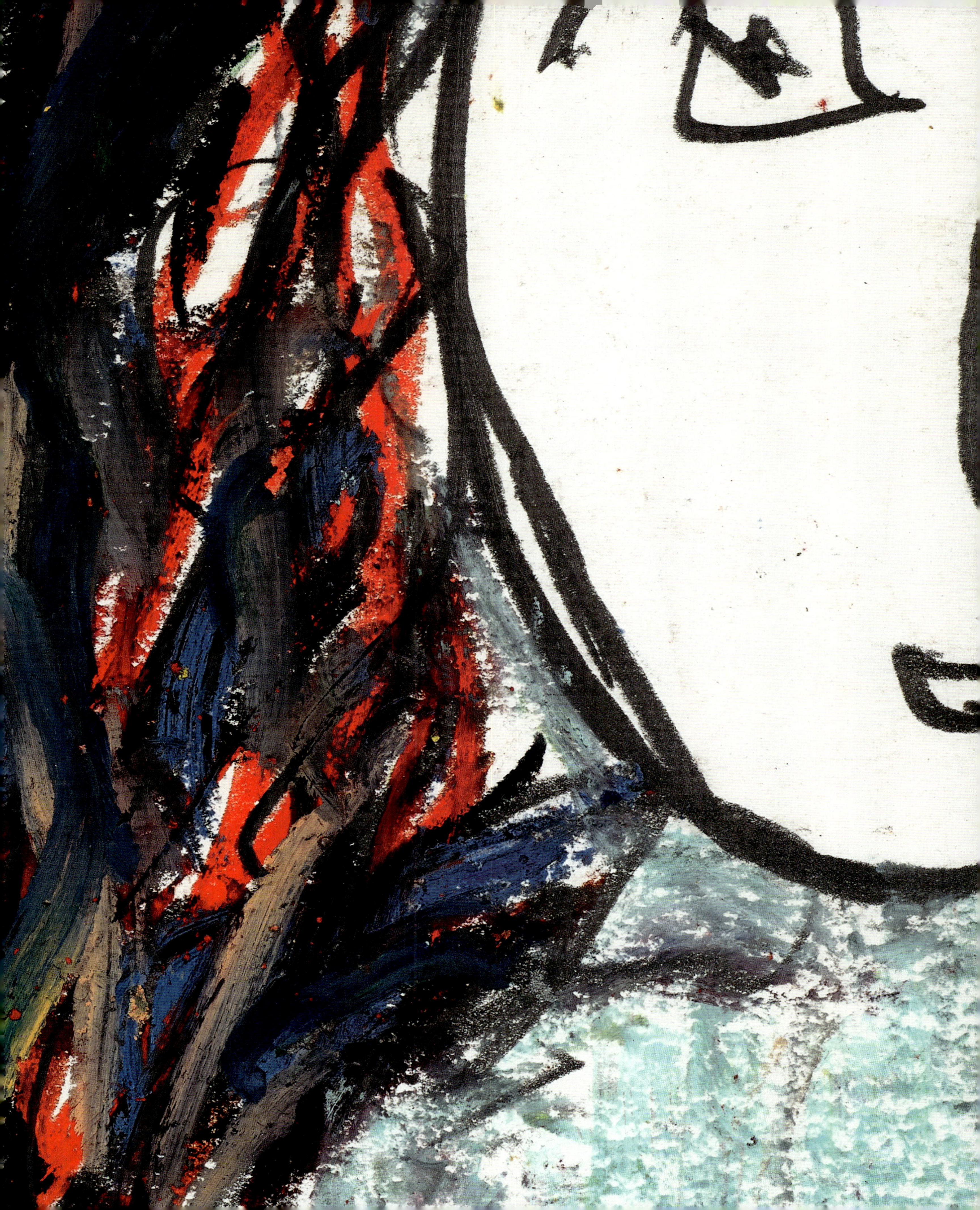

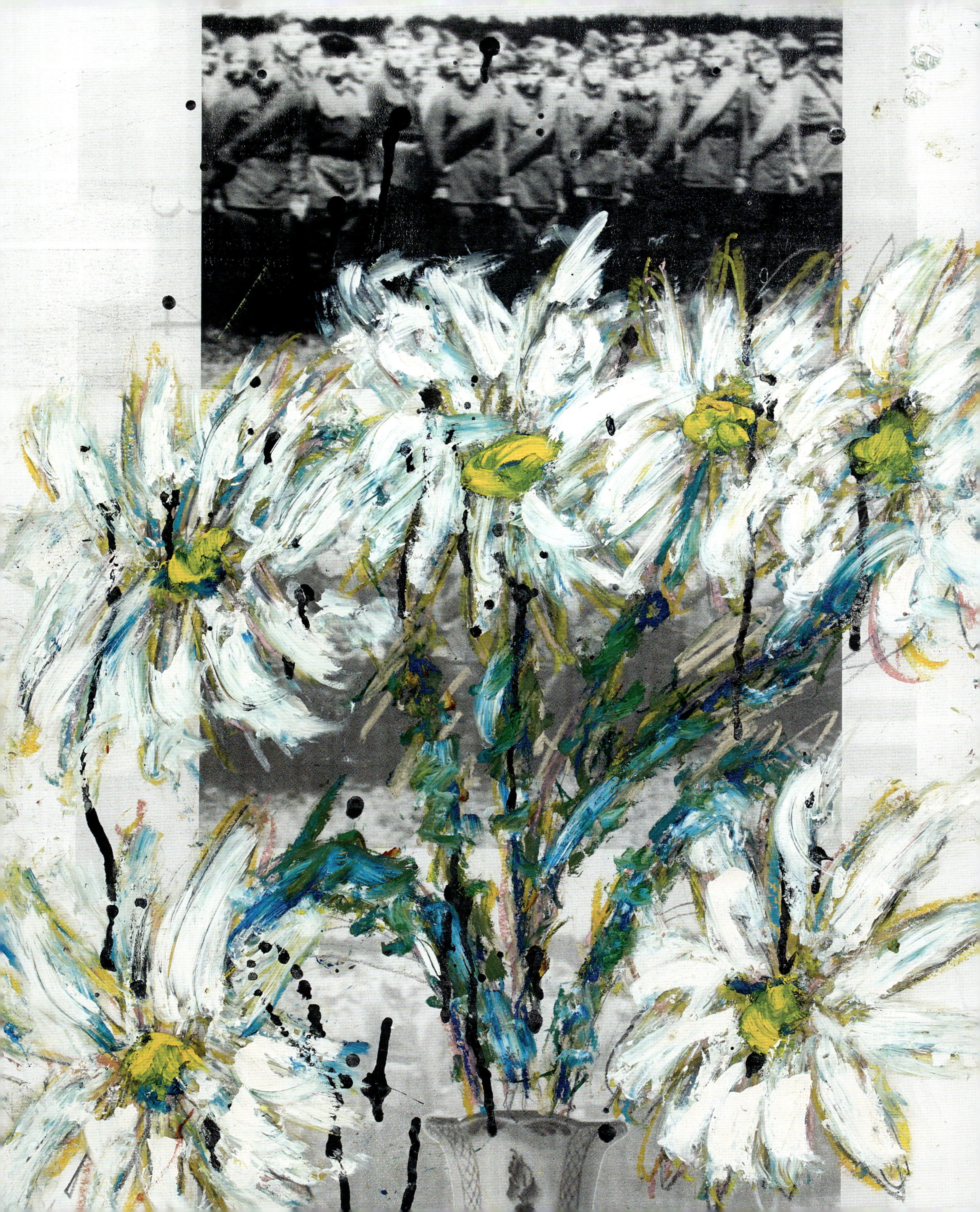

Last March (2007)

John Cauman

A series of 30 works
Digital prints & oil sticks on paper

Naum Medovoy was born in Ukraine, where he lived with his family until the outbreak of World War II. Although he was then but three years old, the war would be the formative experience of his life. His father was mobilized and his family sustained great losses, both on and off the battlefield.

Medovoy studied technical drawing and industrial design and then attended film school. He apprenticed to the director Grigory Chukhray, for whom he researched and selected documentary materials, and he later did similar work for the director Elem Klimov. He established his own career as a documentary filmmaker with a series of short films for television, culminating in the 25-minute film *The Missing (The Last March)*, completed in 1972.

The Last March reveals some of the little-known history of World War II. Few in the West are aware of the extent of the Soviets' sacrifice, estimated at over 25 million deaths, civilian and military. The central theme of *The Last March* is a massive cruelty of which many—even in Russia—are unaware: the film documents the fate of Soviet soldiers who survived capture by the Germans and were released at war's end in 1945, only to be designated traitors by Stalin and sent to gulags in Siberia.

In 1976 Medovoy emigrated to the United States and began a second career as a visual artist. Although in the Soviet Union he had seen the burgeoning of the Non-Conformist art movement challenge the state-sanctioned style of Socialist Realism, the widespread freedom of American art—the liberating expressiveness of Willem de Kooning and Jackson Pollock, the overtly popular imagery of Andy Warhol and Jasper Johns—came as a revelation to him. He began to draw in a loose, coloristic, expressive style, which for him was a means of conveying both the exhilaration and the tragedy that encompassed his experience as an artist and as a citizen.

Last March, a series of works on paper Medovoy completed in 2007, synthesizes his bifurcated life: Russian and American, filmmaker and painter. The series comprises a theme with variations. The prototype is three horizontal bands of a photographic image, a digital print in black-and-white derived from a sequence in his documentary film *The Last March*; the images fade into decreasing visibility from top to bottom. Overlaid on the photographs are loosely rendered images of flowers, usually emanating from a vase, vividly rendered in primary and secondary colors and often overlaid with expressive drips of paint.

These dual components evoke the human consequences of war as they affect the soldiers in battle and the women who wait for them, the joy of those who return from battle, and the sorrow for those who do not. The flowers—often chamomiles, the Russian national flower—are emblematic of the brevity and vulnerability of life on earth. As Vitaly Komar has noted, Medovoy's fragments of documentary images "enter into a moving dialogue with the colorful 'explosions' of his bouquets of expressionism." These dialogues vary in emotional pitch, like movements in a symphony. They are, variously, harmonious and contrapuntal, still and cacophonous, solemn and joyous. Sometimes the bouquets seem to drape the images, as in *Last March 6*; at other times they nearly obliterate them, as in *Last March 9*. Medovoy's series fulfills the dictum of the Latvian-born American painter Mark Rothko, who asserted that the subject matter of art should be both "tragic and timeless."

Last March 36, 2007 (detail)

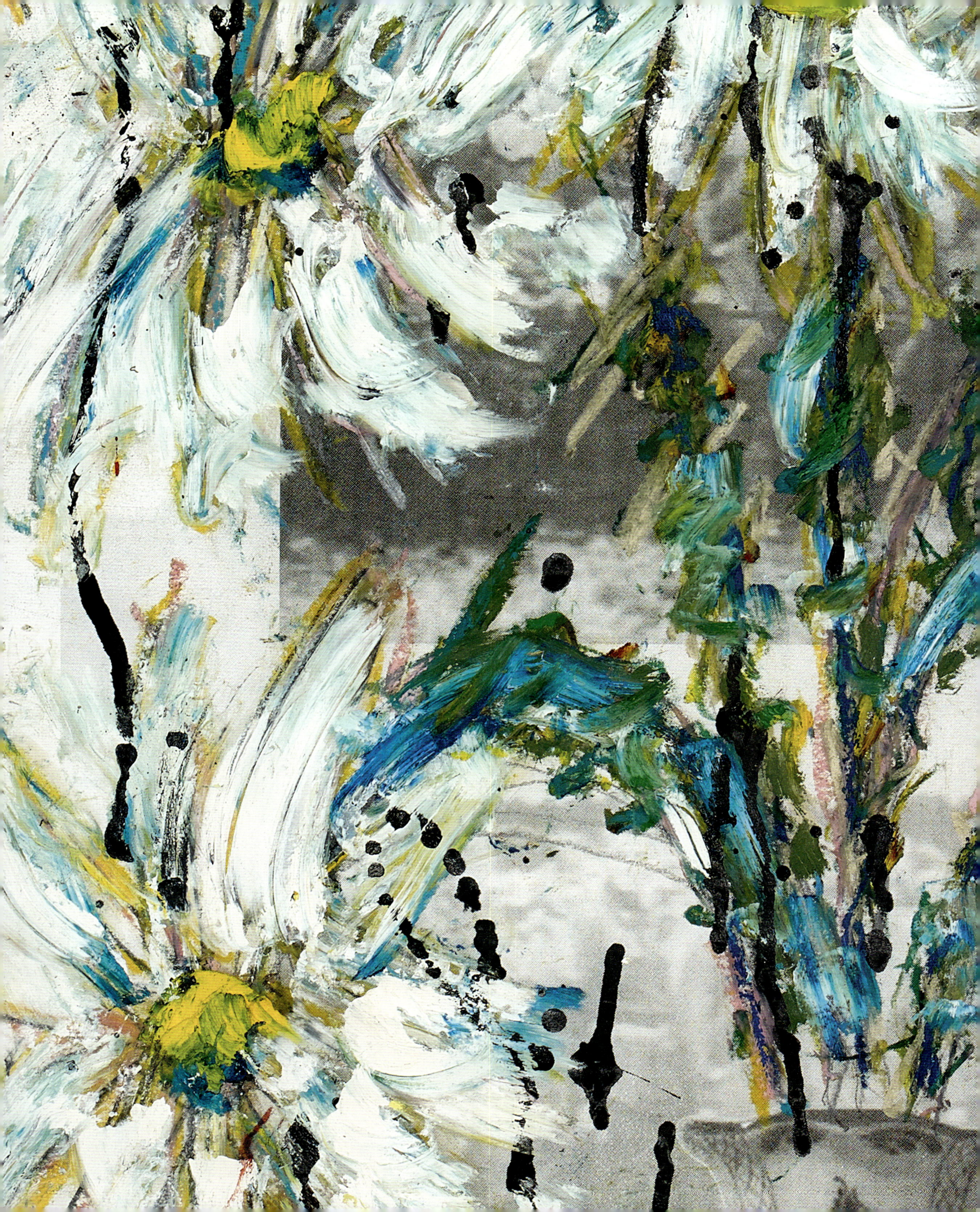

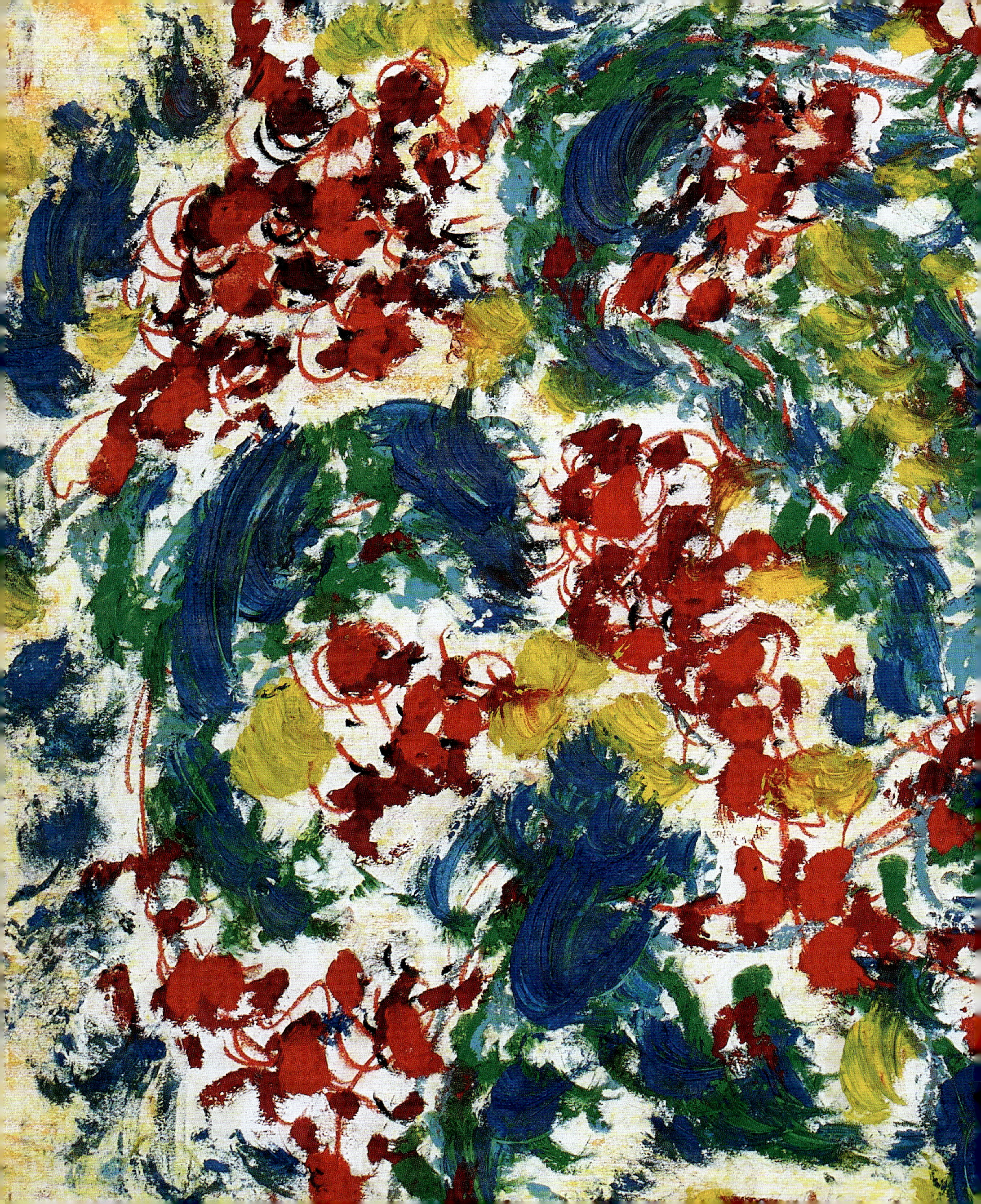

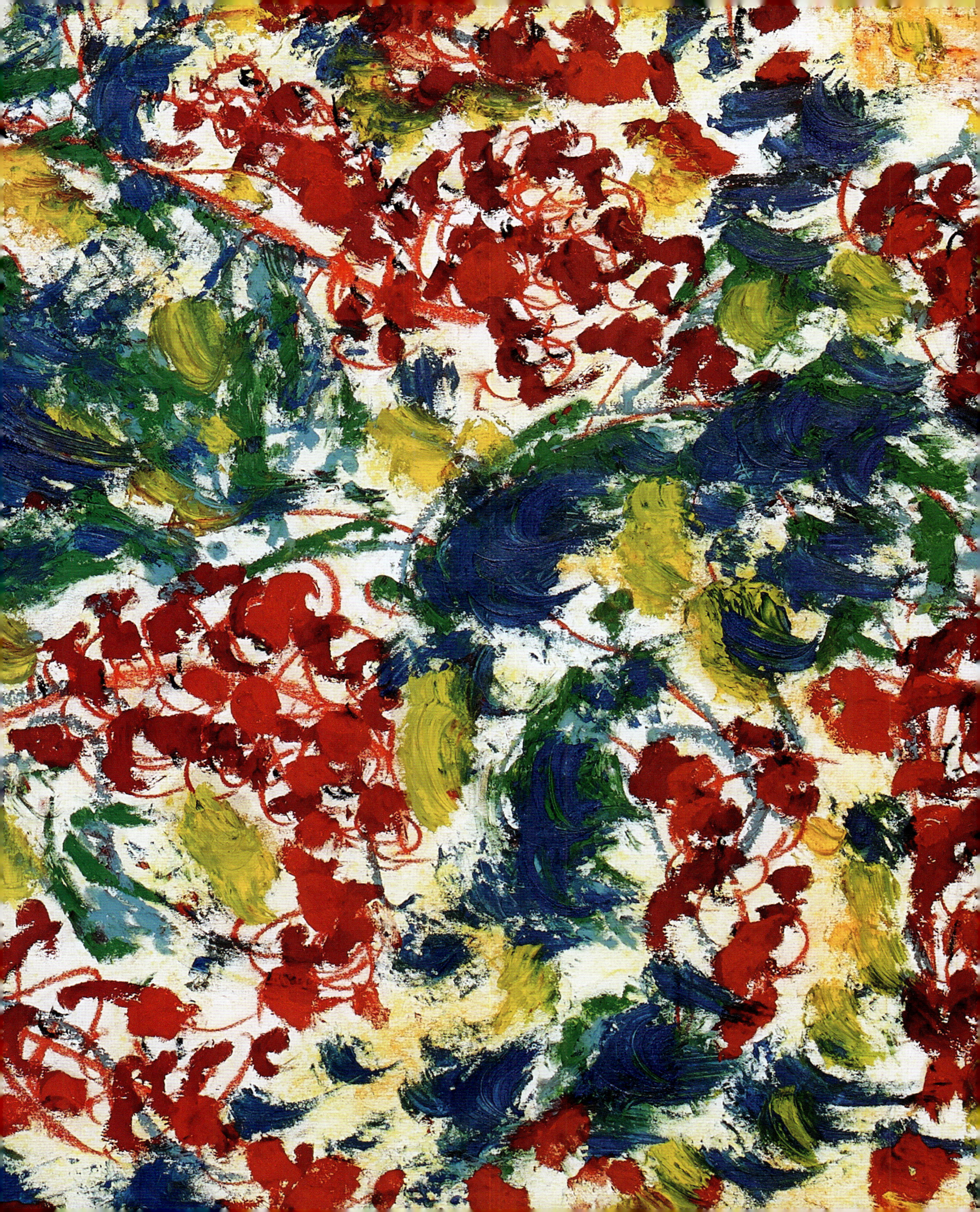

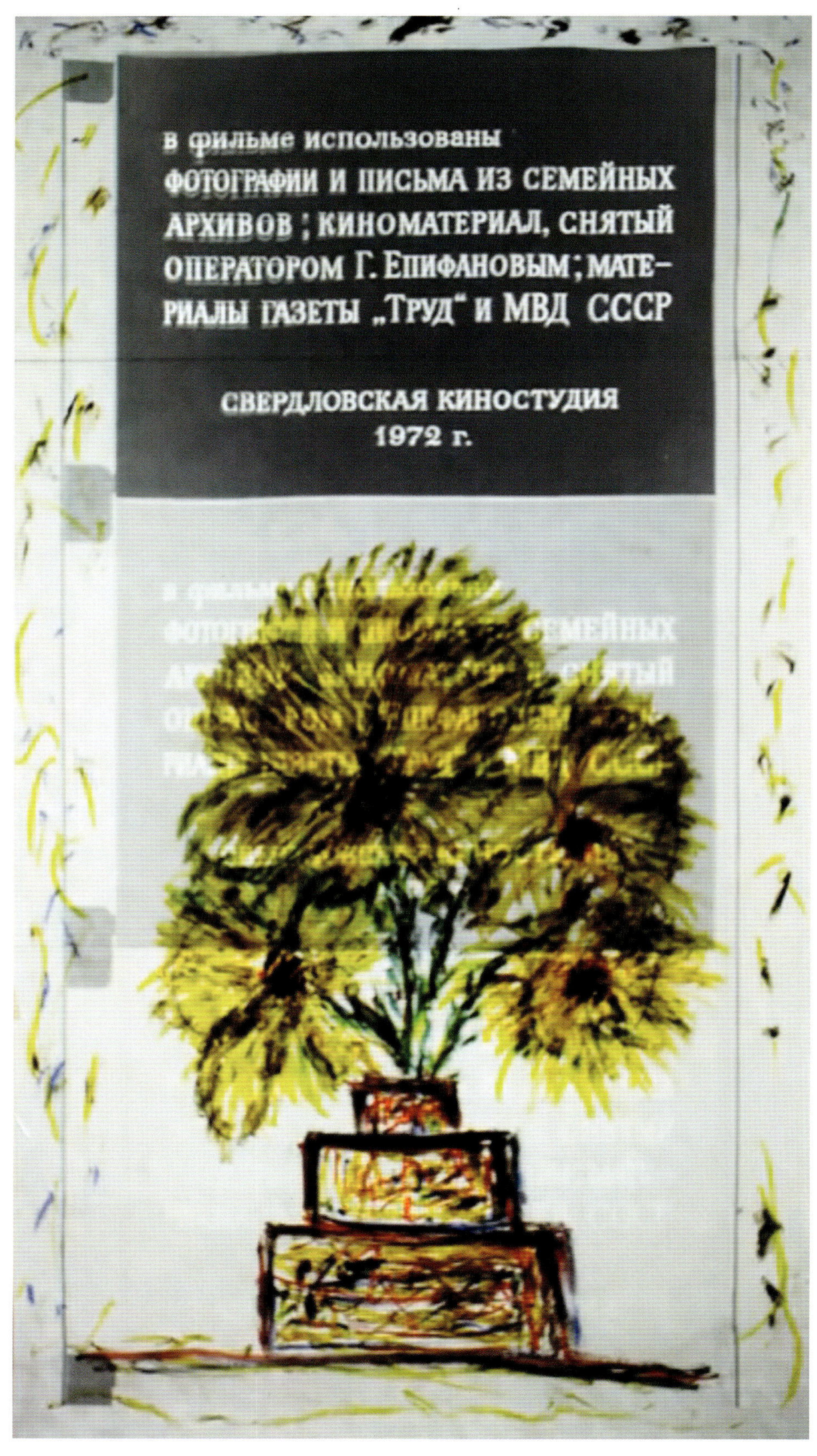

pp. 32–33
Last March 39, 2007 (detail)
Digital print, oil sticks on paper

Trevor Tweeten and Naum Medovoy,
The Missing (The Last March), 2014,
still (detail)

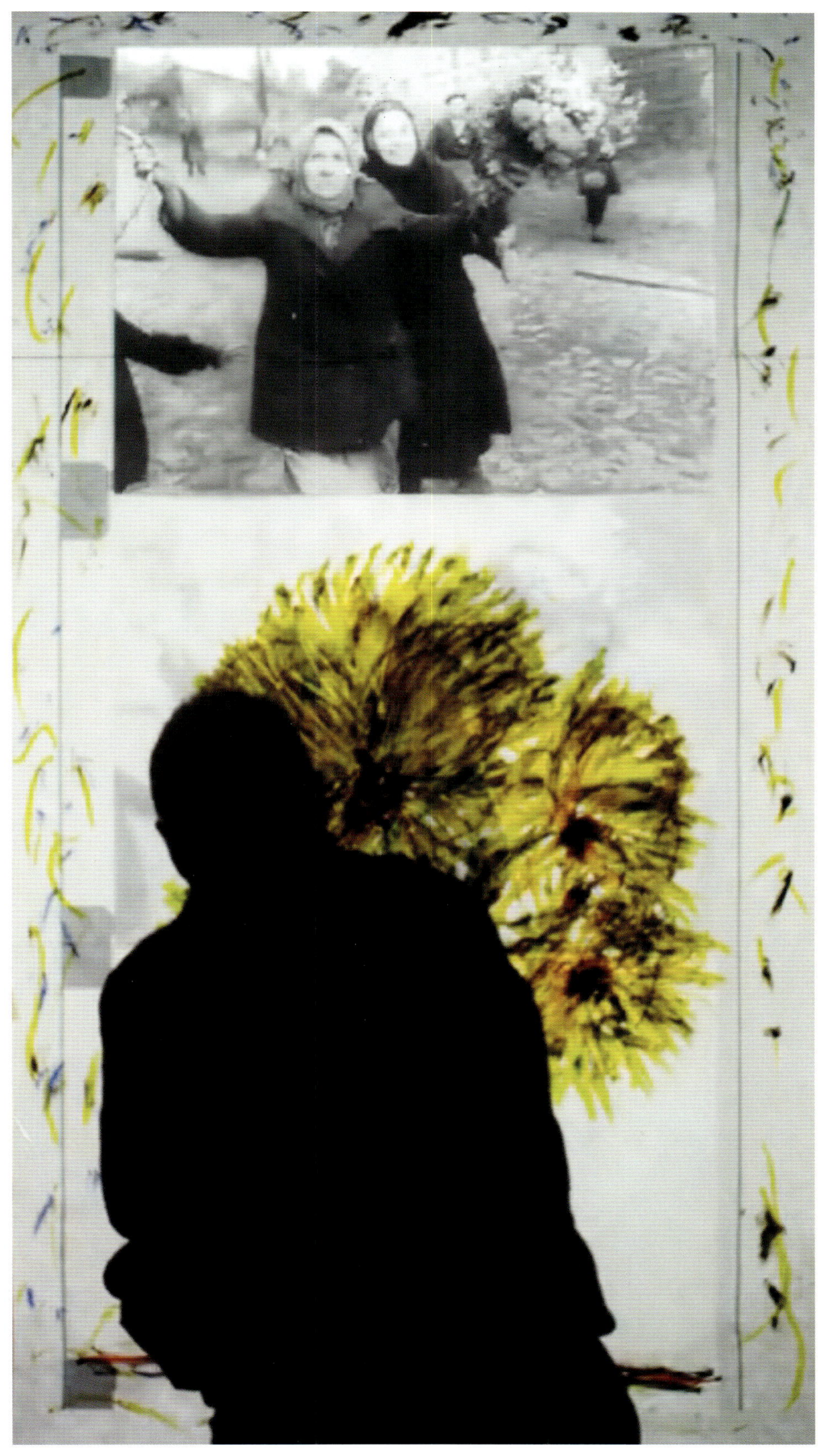

Trevor Tweeten and Naum Medovoy, *The Missing (The Last March)*, 2014, still (detail)

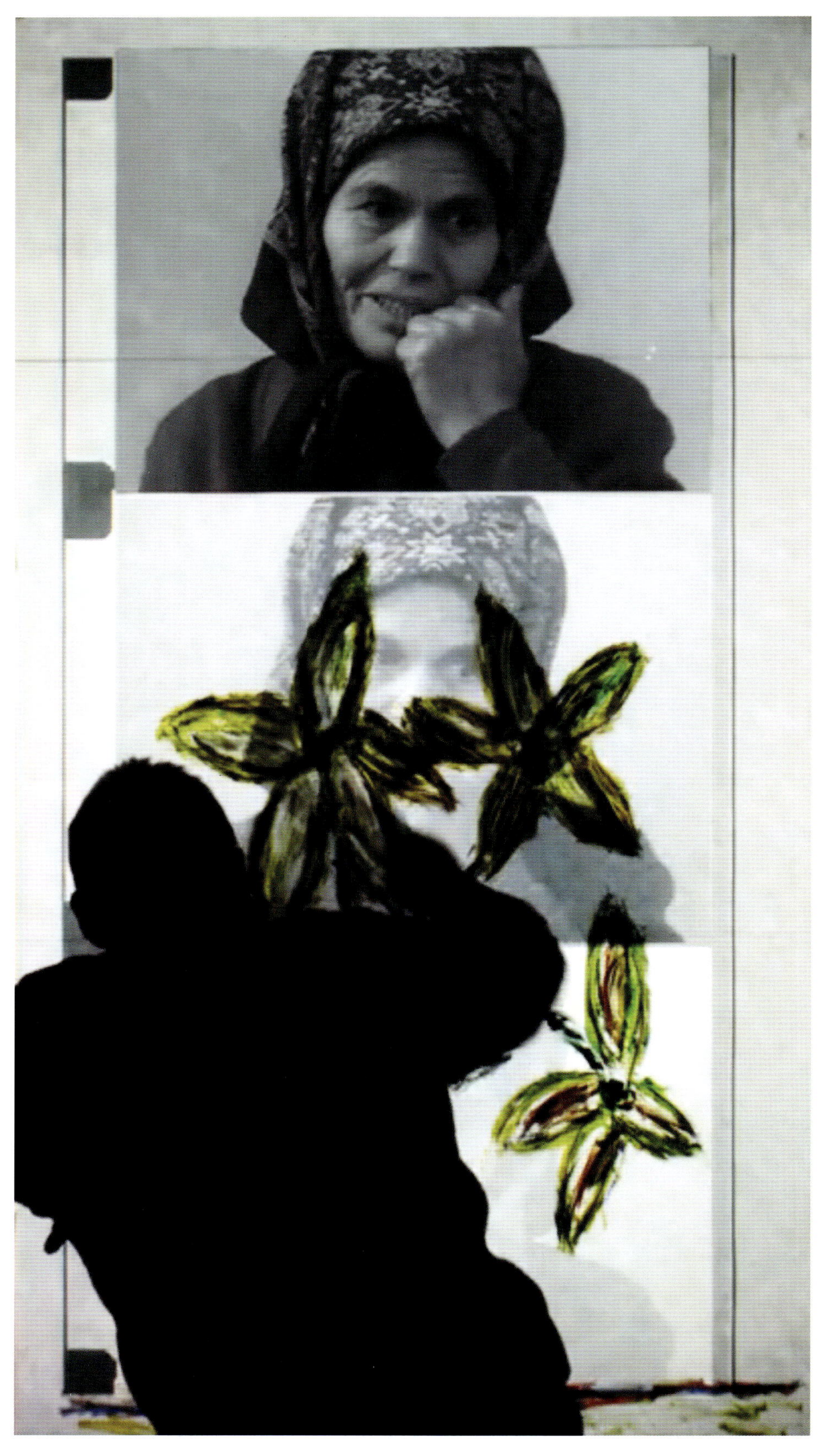

Trevor Tweeten and Naum Medovoy, *The Missing
(The Last March)*, 2014, still (detail)

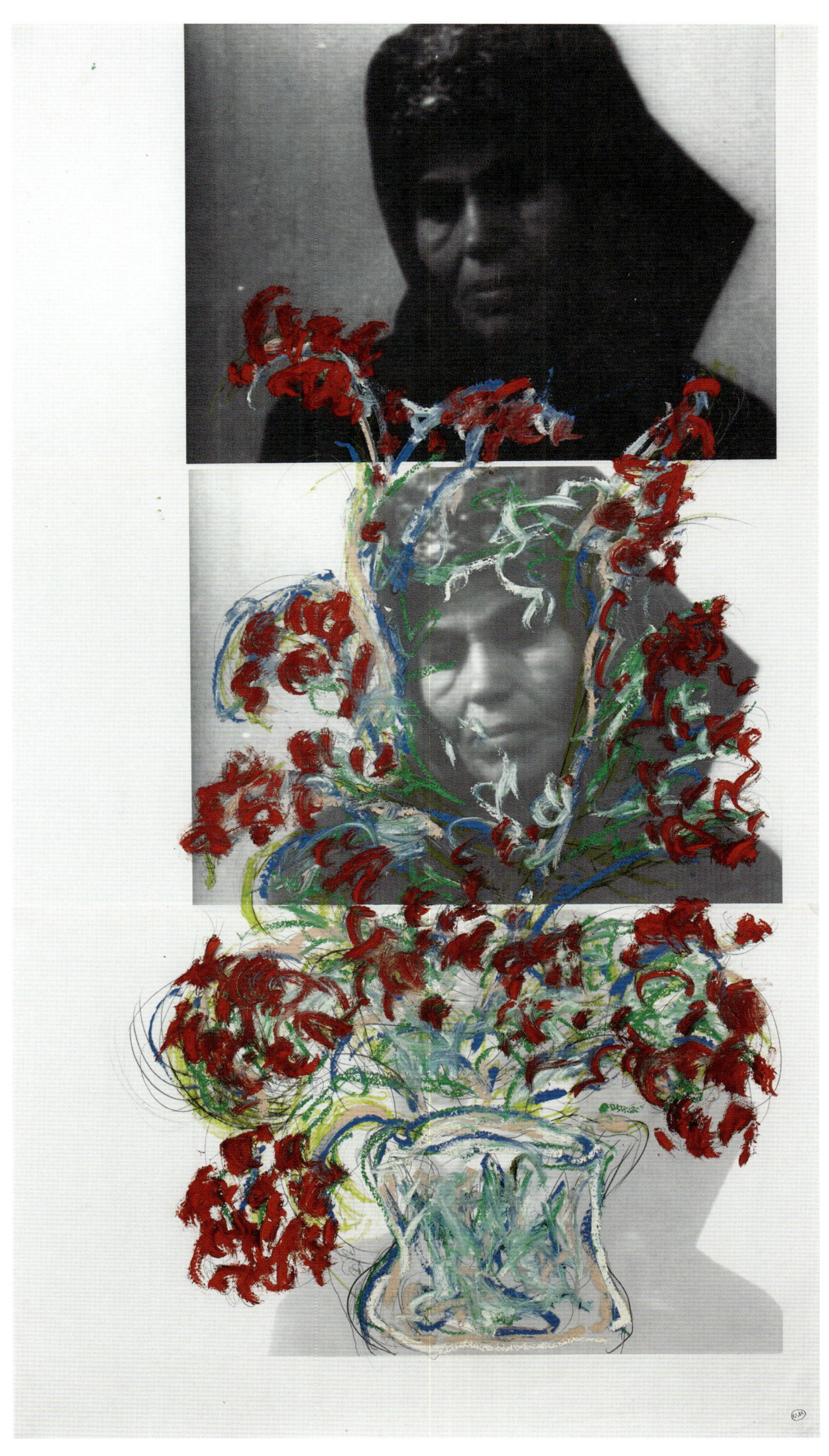

Last March 19, 2007
Digital print, oil sticks on paper,
62 ½ x 36 in. / 158.75 x 91.44 cm

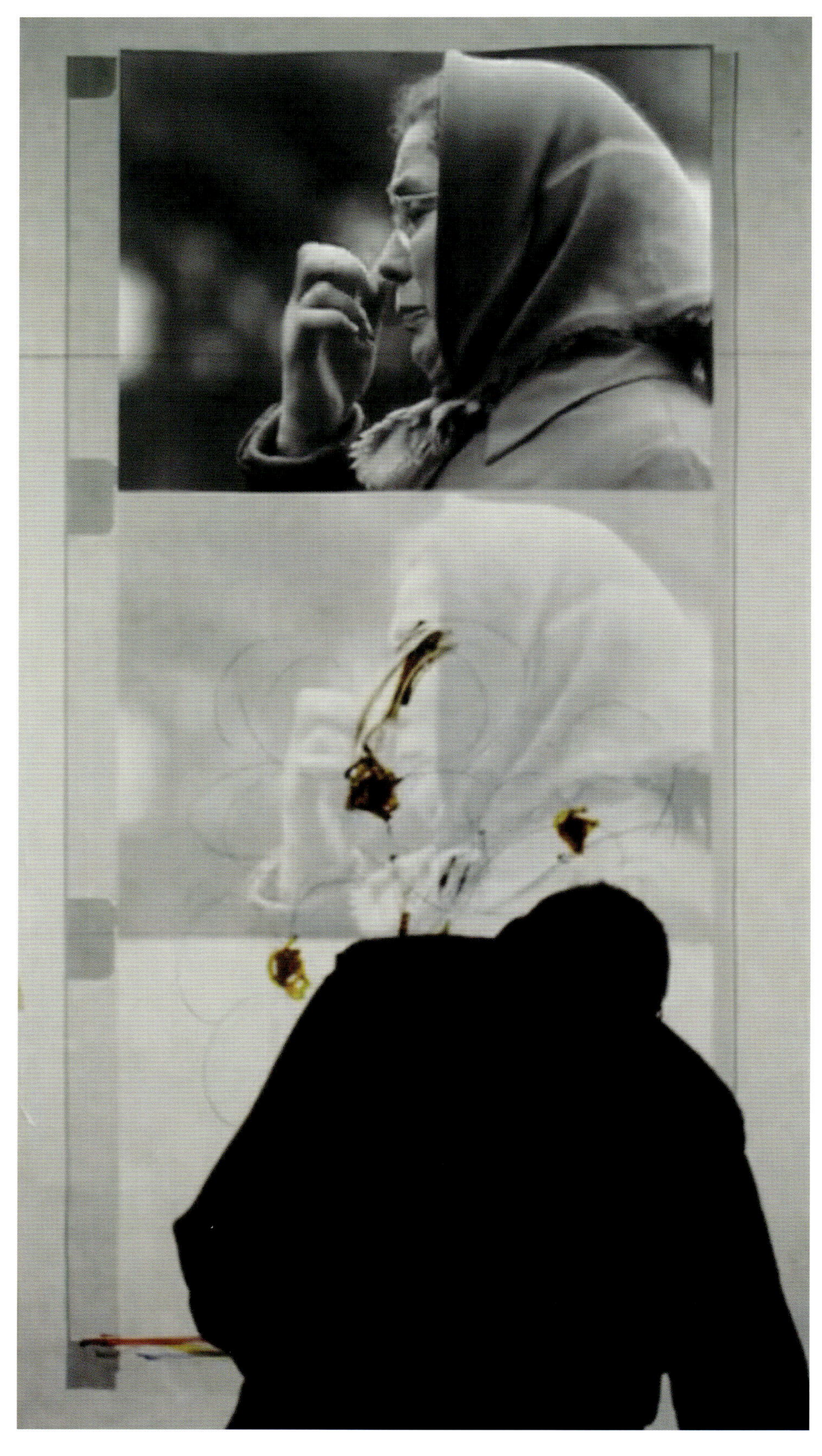

Trevor Tweeten and Naum Medovoy, *The Missing (The Last March)*, 2014, still (detail)

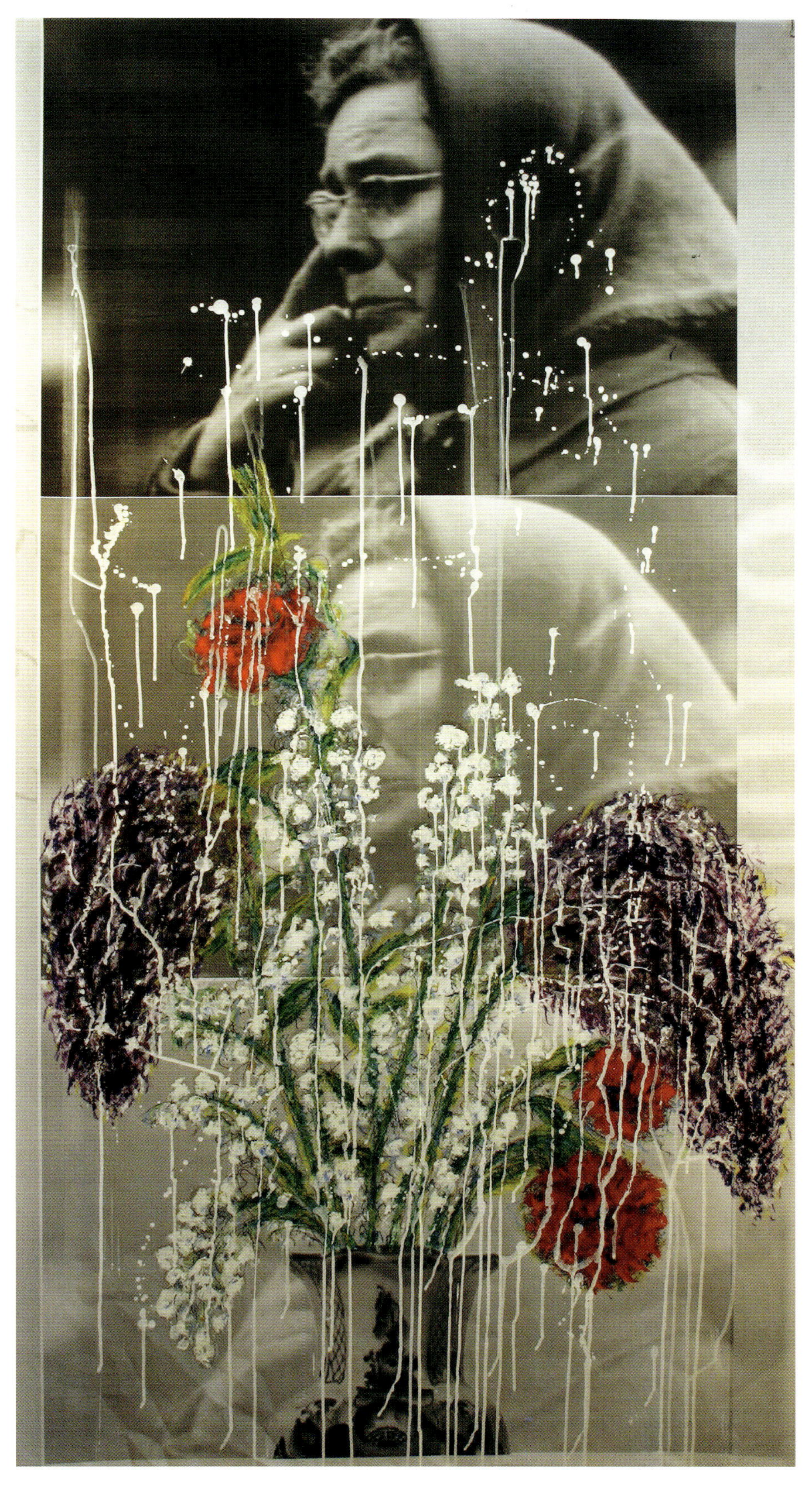

Last March 27, 2007
Digital print, oil sticks on paper,
65 ½ x 36 in. / 166.37 x 60.96 cm

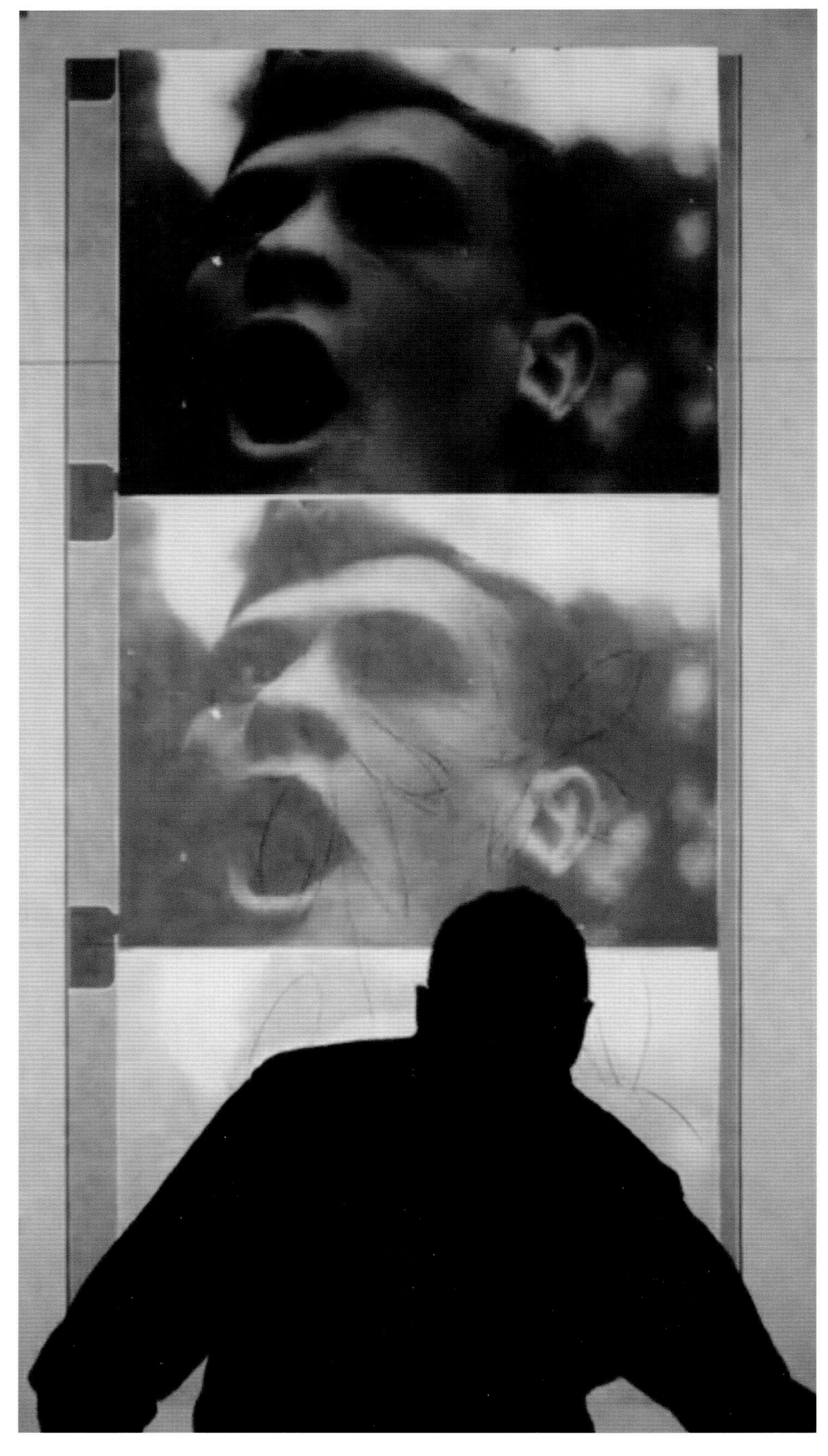

Trevor Tweeten and Naum Medovoy, *The Missing*
(The Last March), 2014, still (detail)

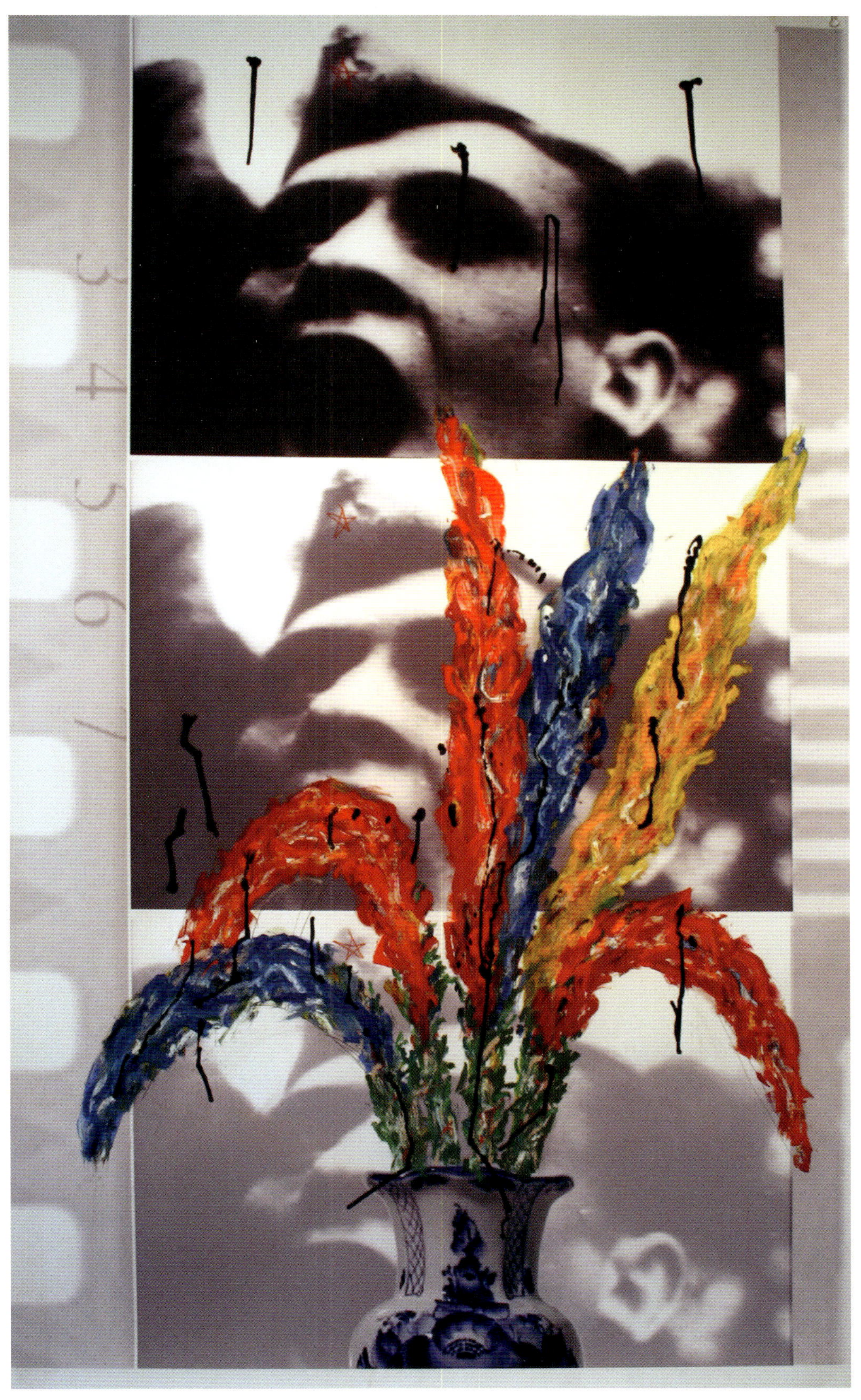

Last March 33, 2007
Digital print, oil sticks on paper,
66 ½ x 39 in. / 168.91 x 99.06 cm

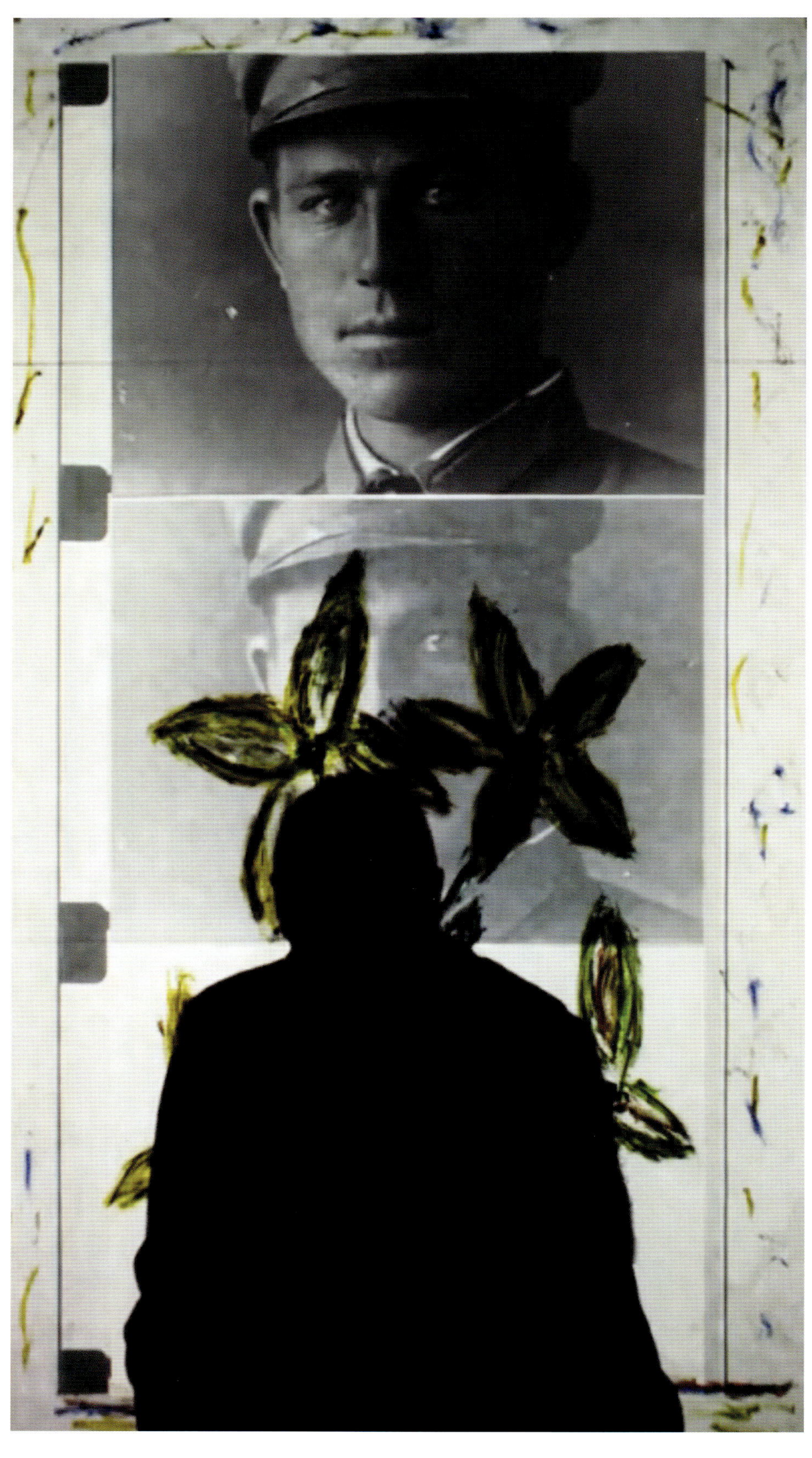

Trevor Tweeten and Naum Medovoy, *The Missing*
(*The Last March*), 2014, still (detail)

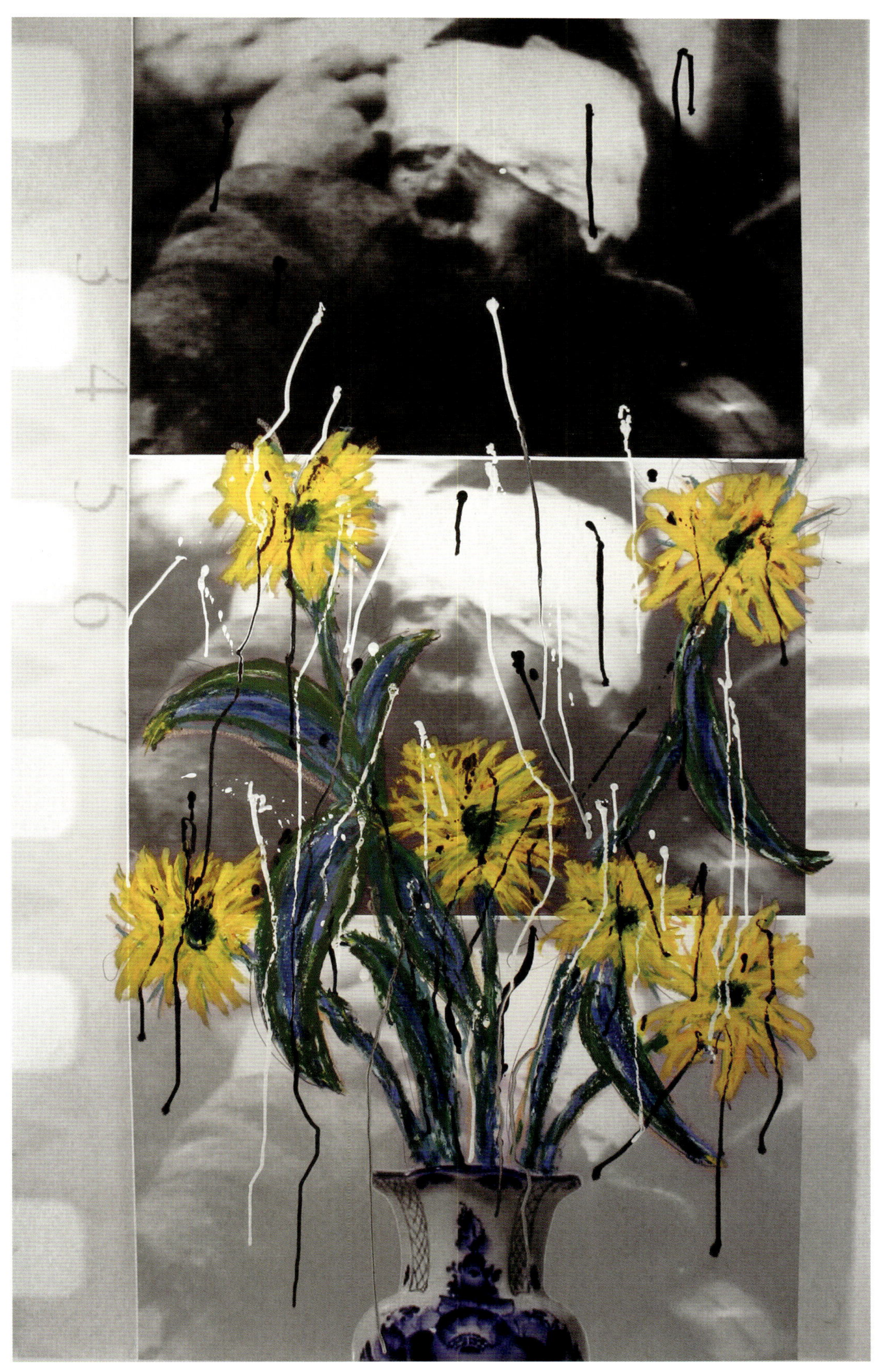

Last March 31, 2007
Digital print, oil sticks on paper,
66 x 39 in. / 167.64 x 99.06 cm

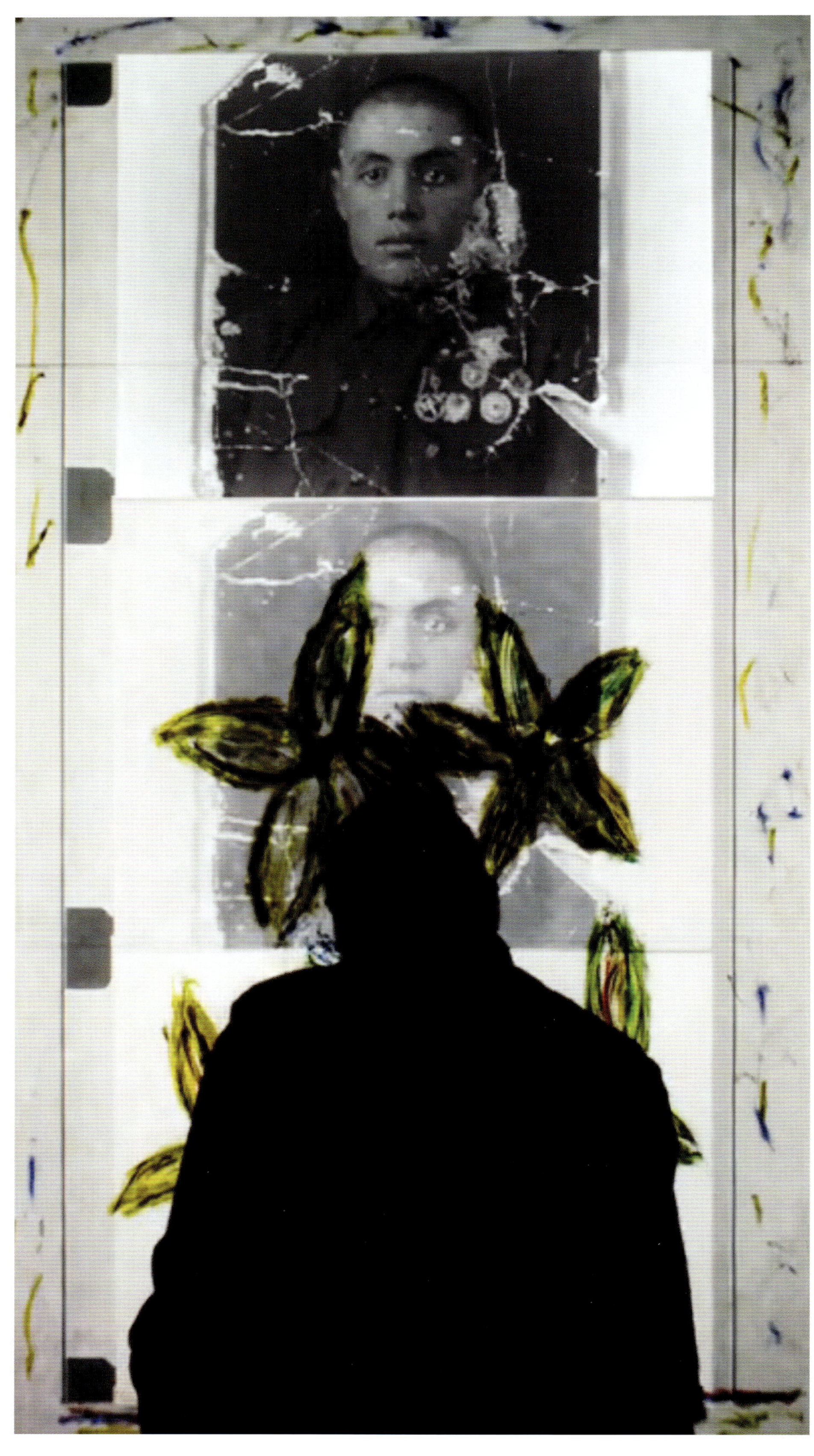

Trevor Tweeten and Naum Medovoy, *The Missing*
(The Last March), 2014, still (detail)

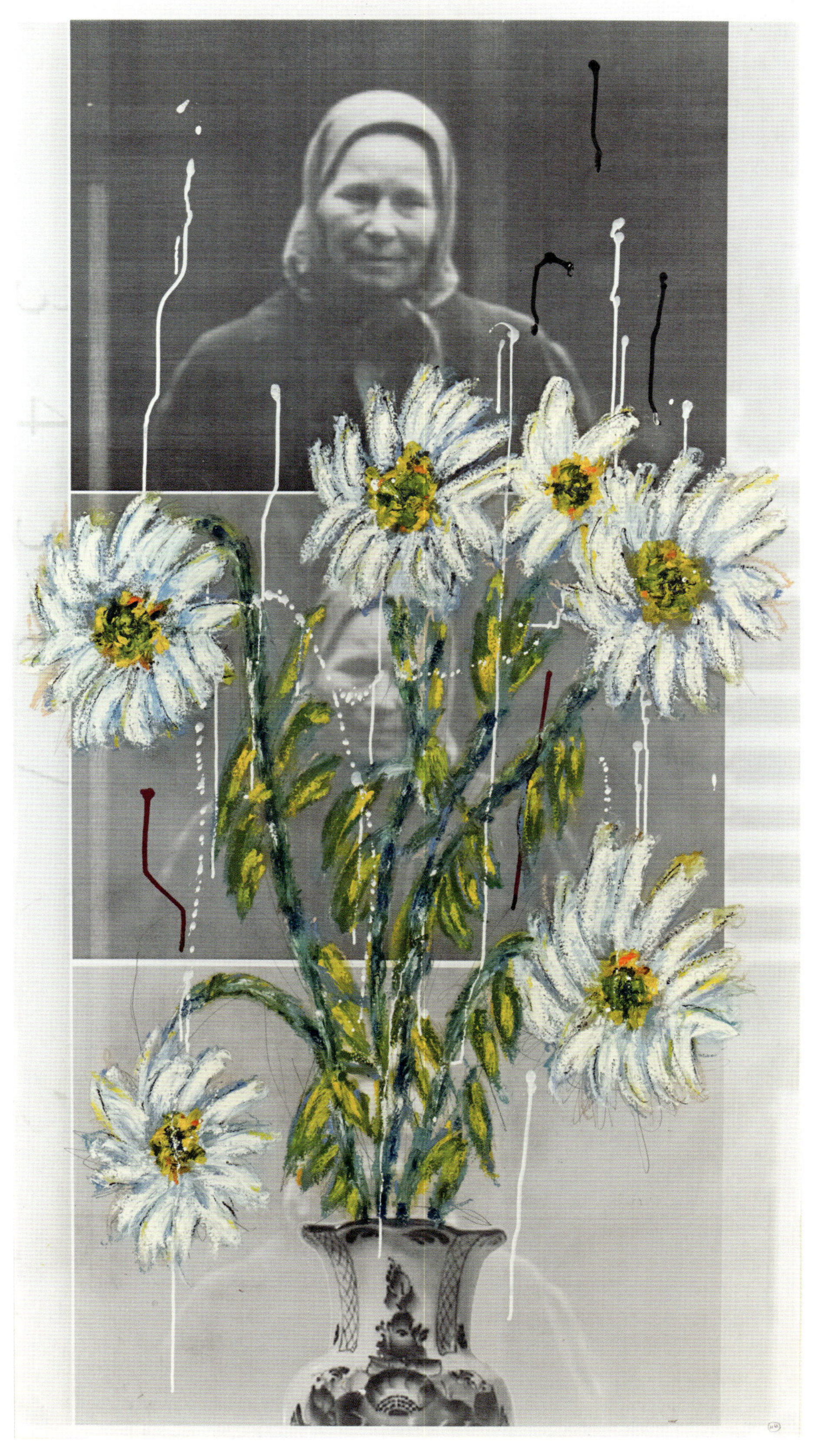

Last March 25, 2007
Digital print, oil sticks on paper,
65 ½ x 36 in. / 166.37 x 60.96 cm

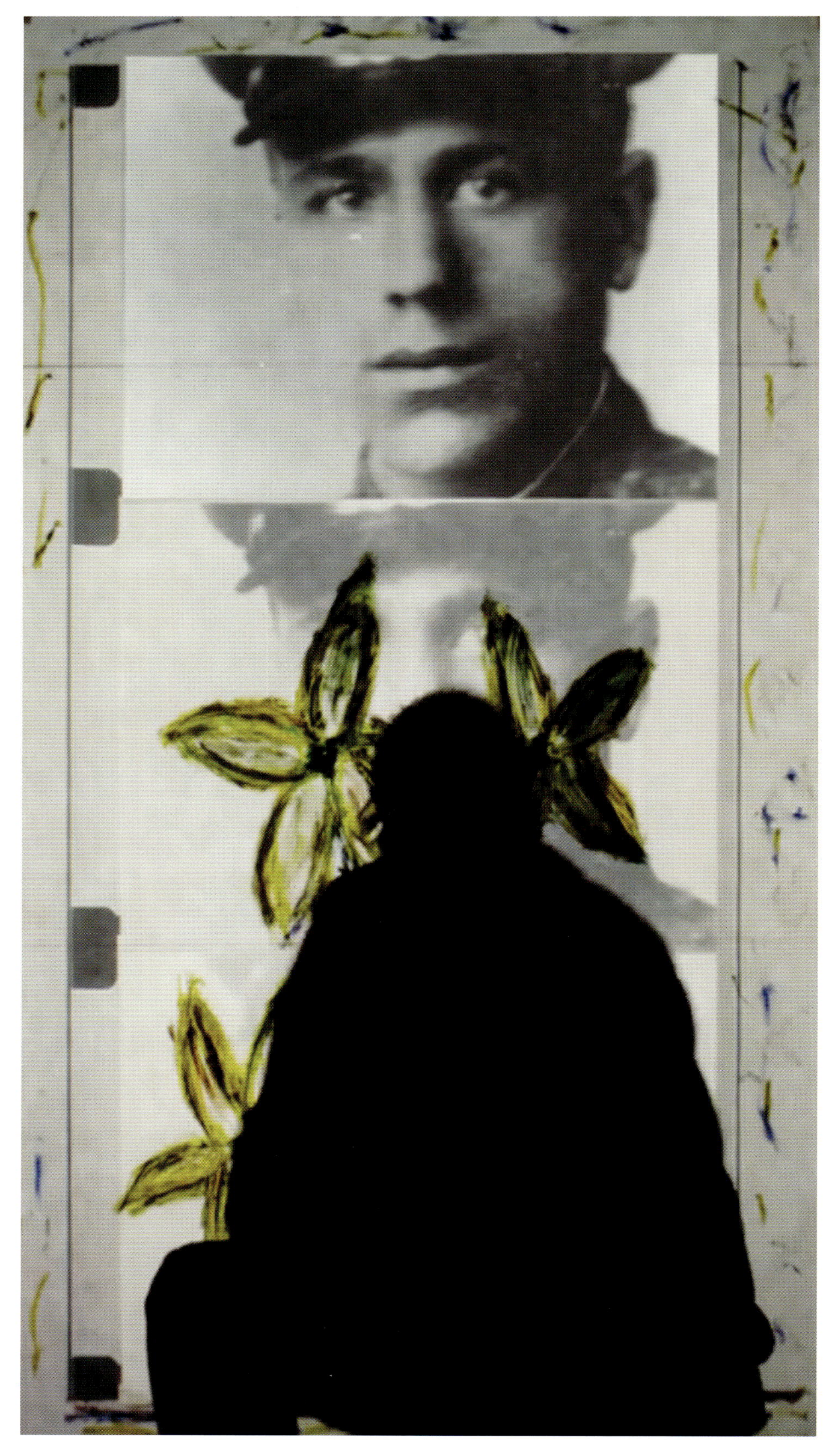

Trevor Tweeten and Naum Medovoy, *The Missing
(The Last March)*, 2014, still (detail)

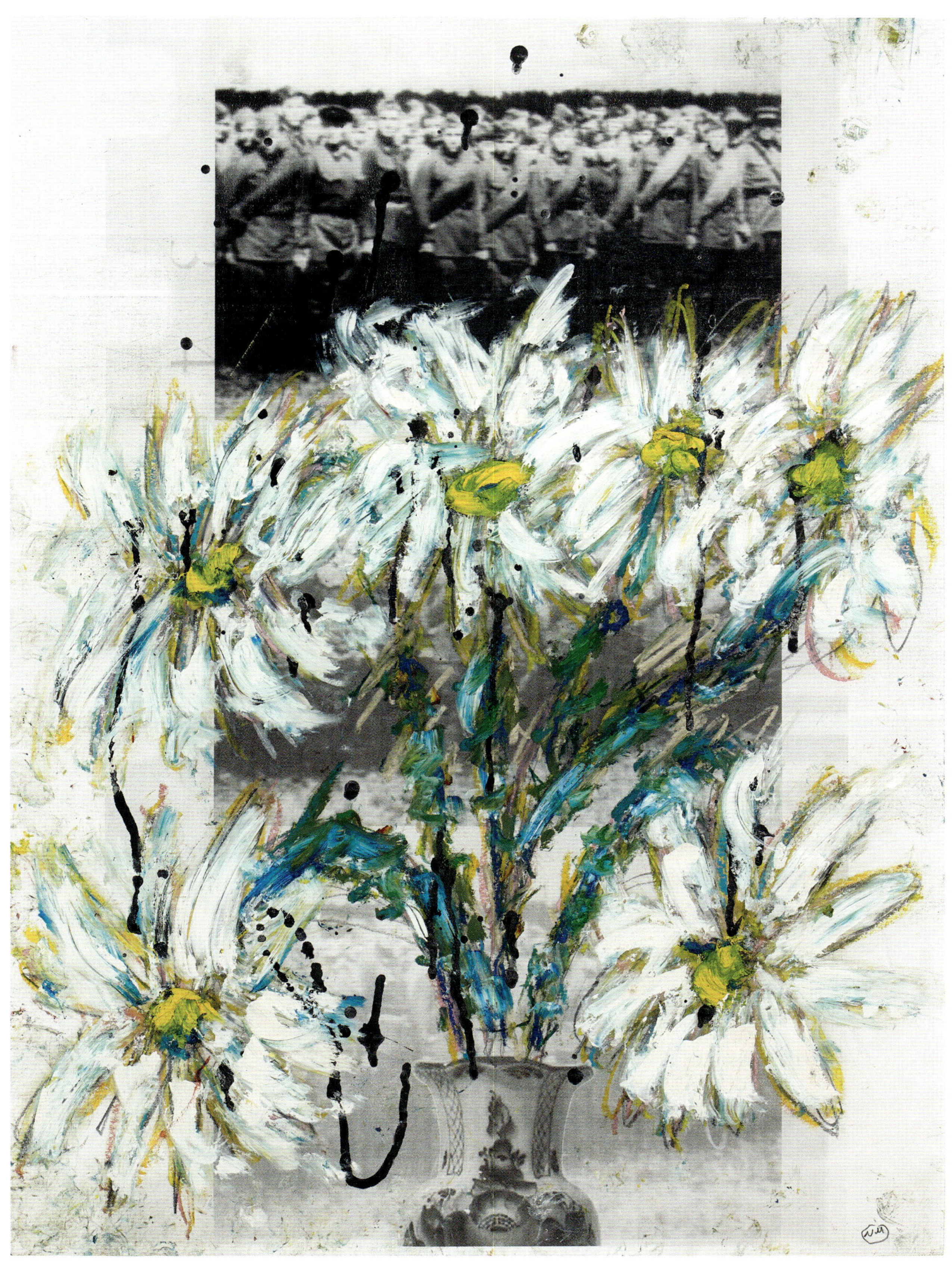

Last March 36, 2007
Digital print, oil sticks on paper,
36 x 24 in. / 91.44 x 60.96 cm

pp. 48–49
Last March 36, 2007 (detail)

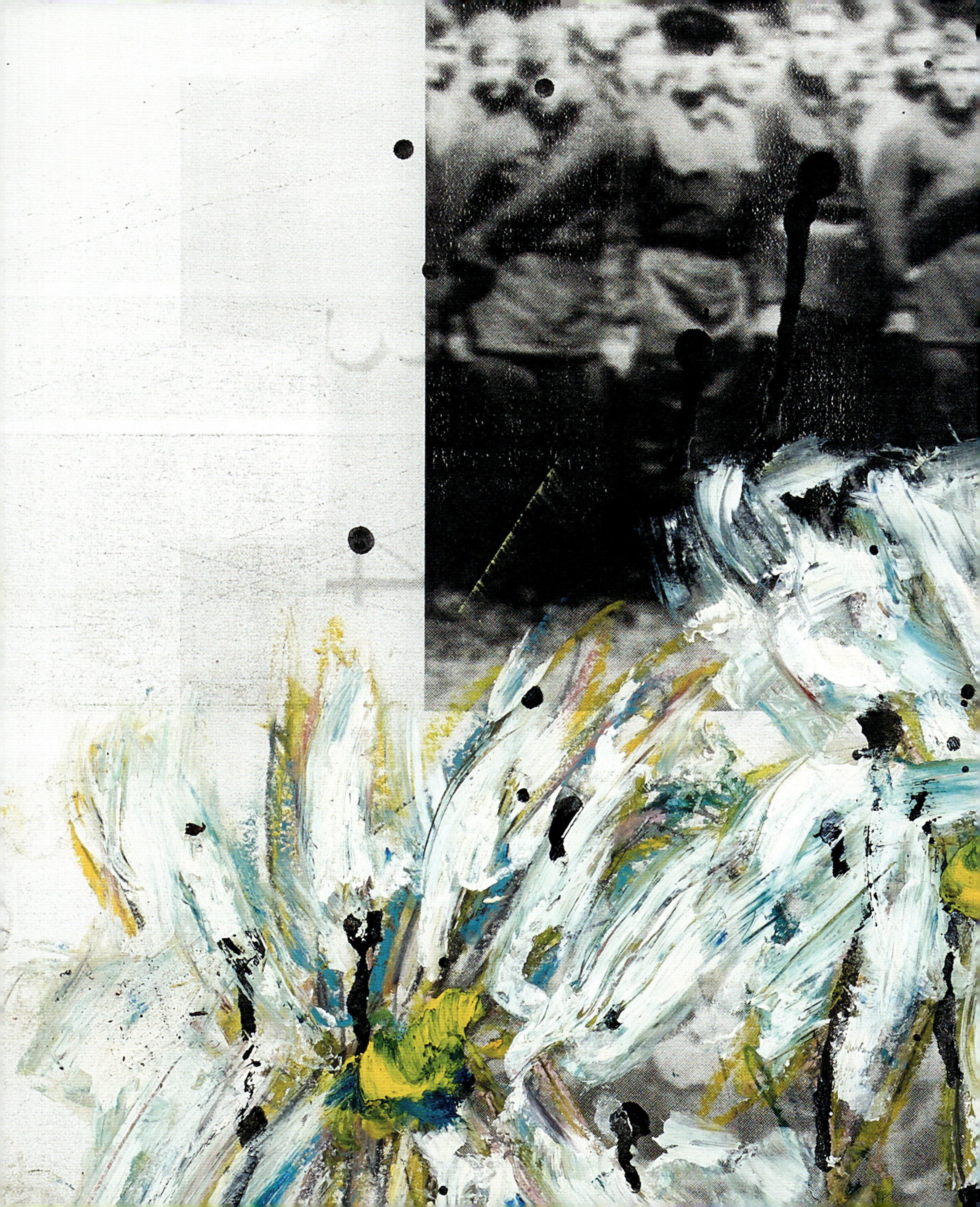

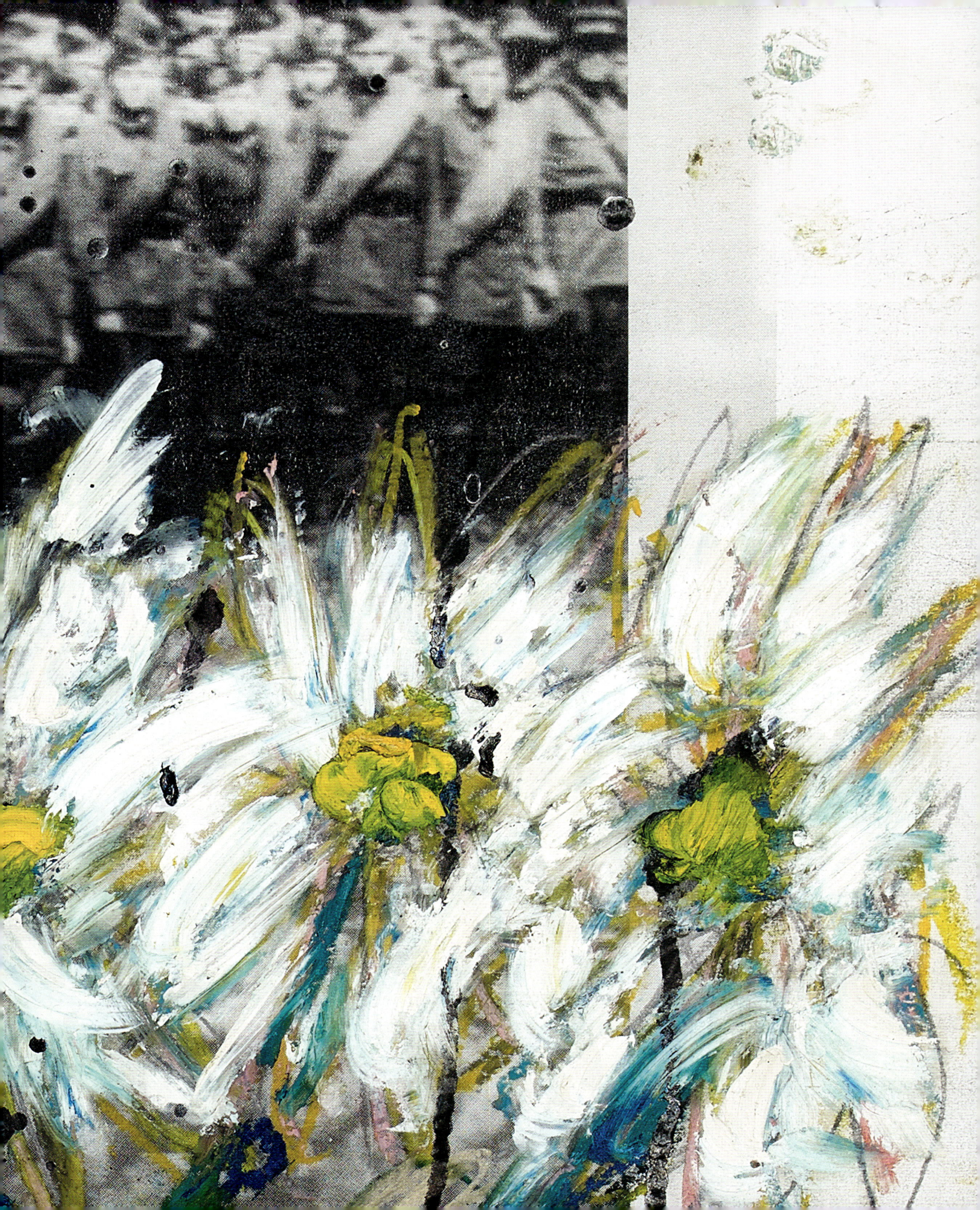

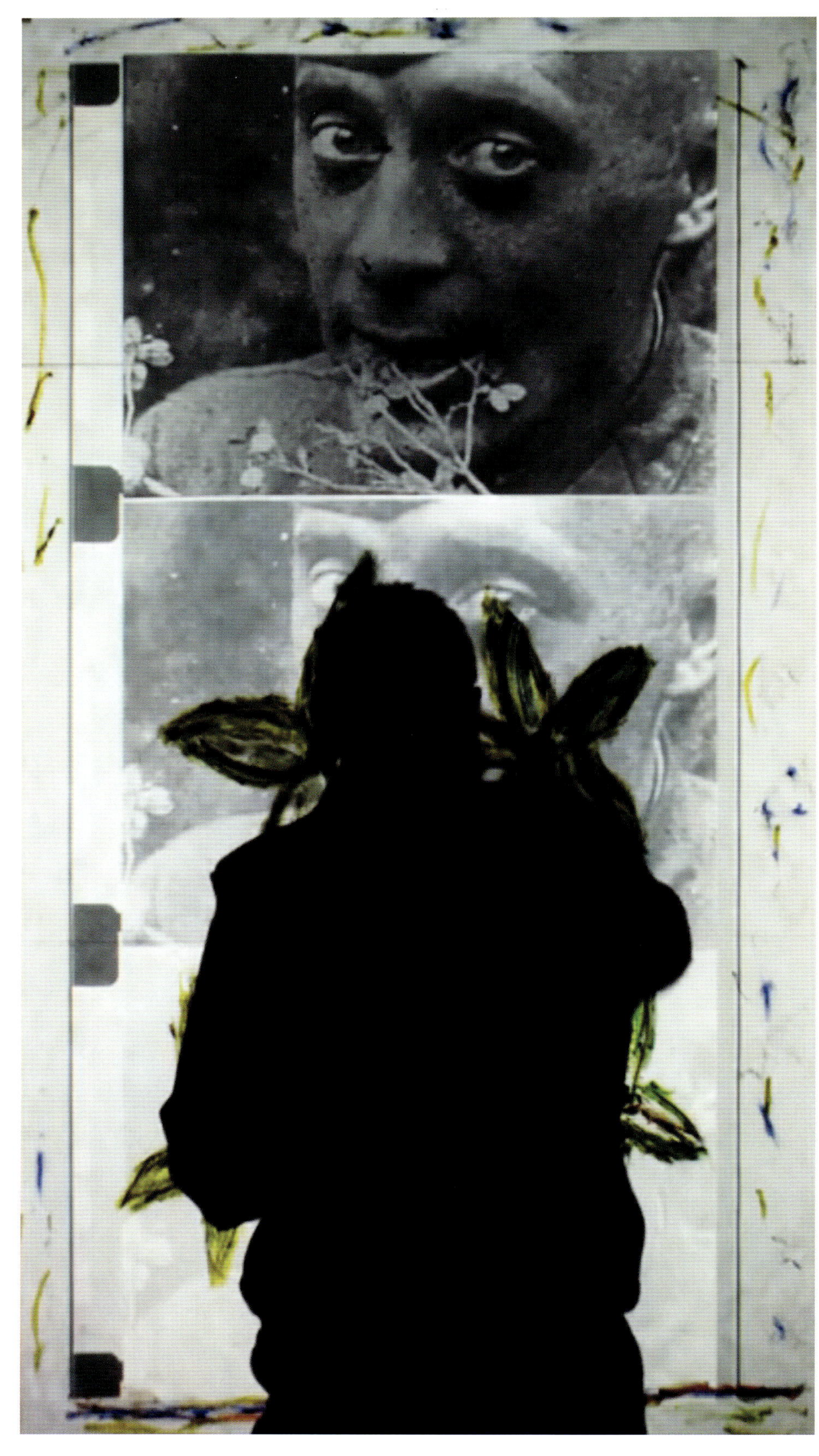

Trevor Tweeten and Naum Medovoy, *The Missing
(The Last March)*, 2014, still (detail)

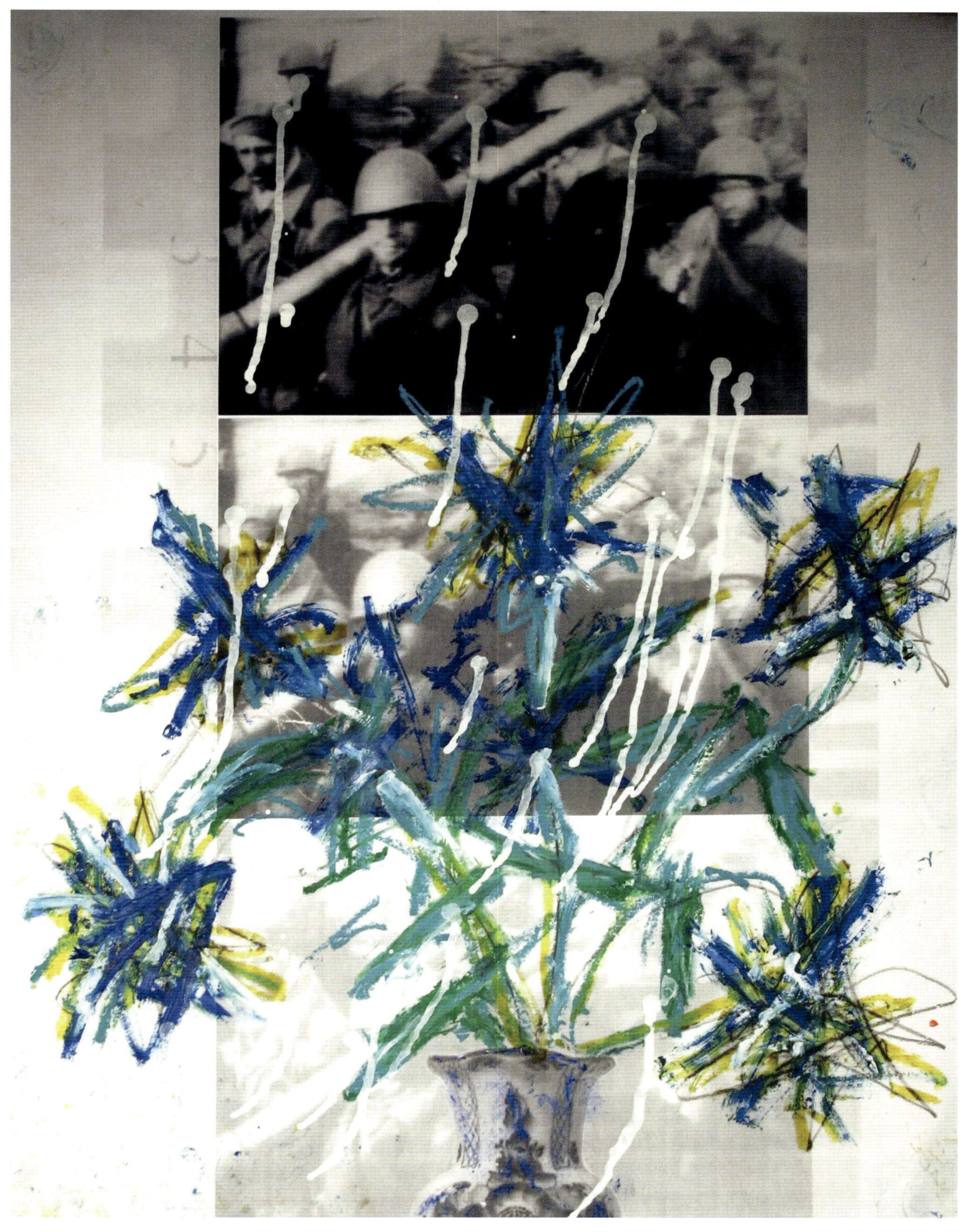

Last March 7, 2007
Digital print, oil sticks on paper,
24 x 18 in. / 60.96 x 45.72 cm

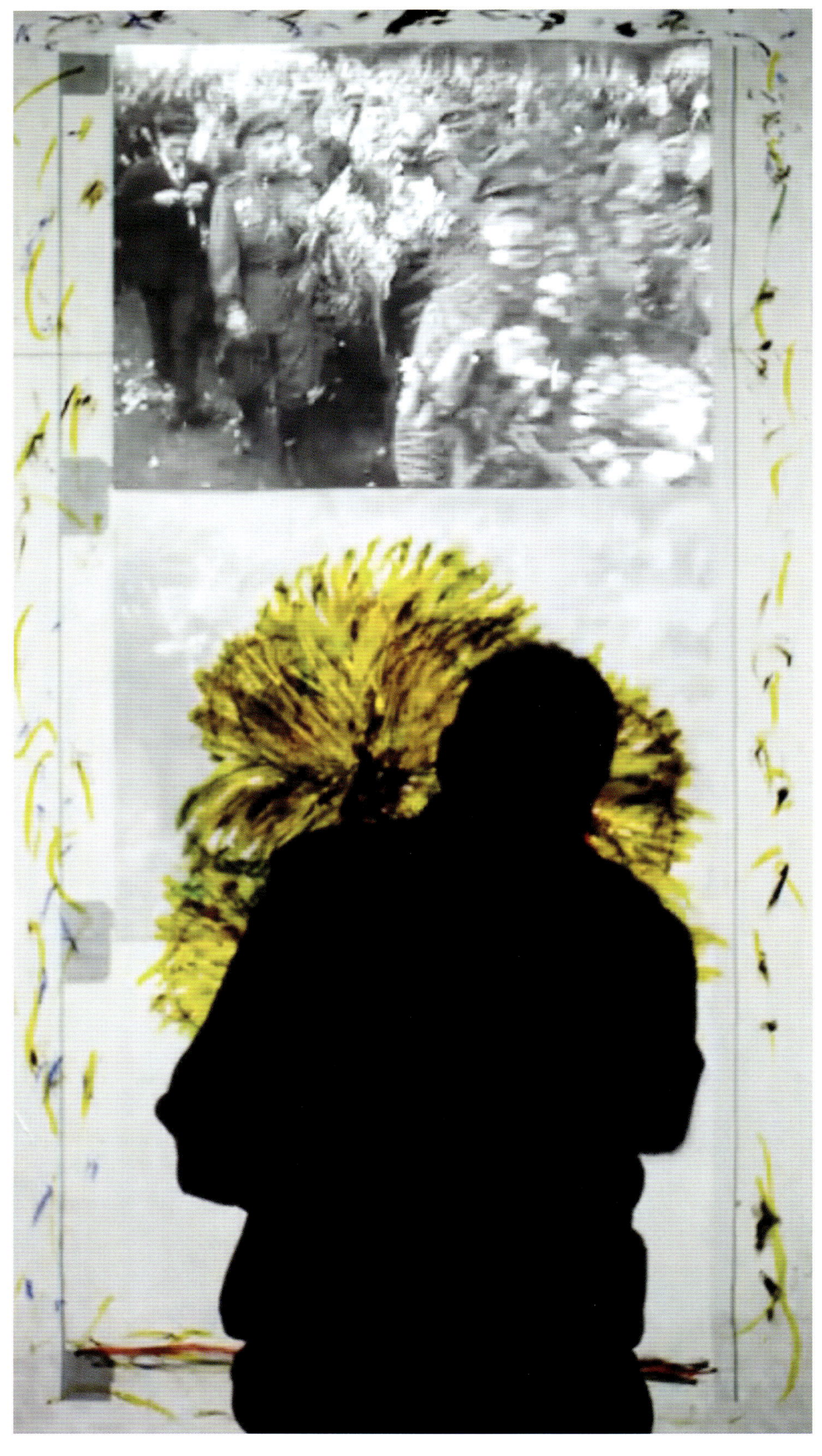

Trevor Tweeten and Naum Medovoy, *The Missing*
(The Last March), 2014, still (detail)

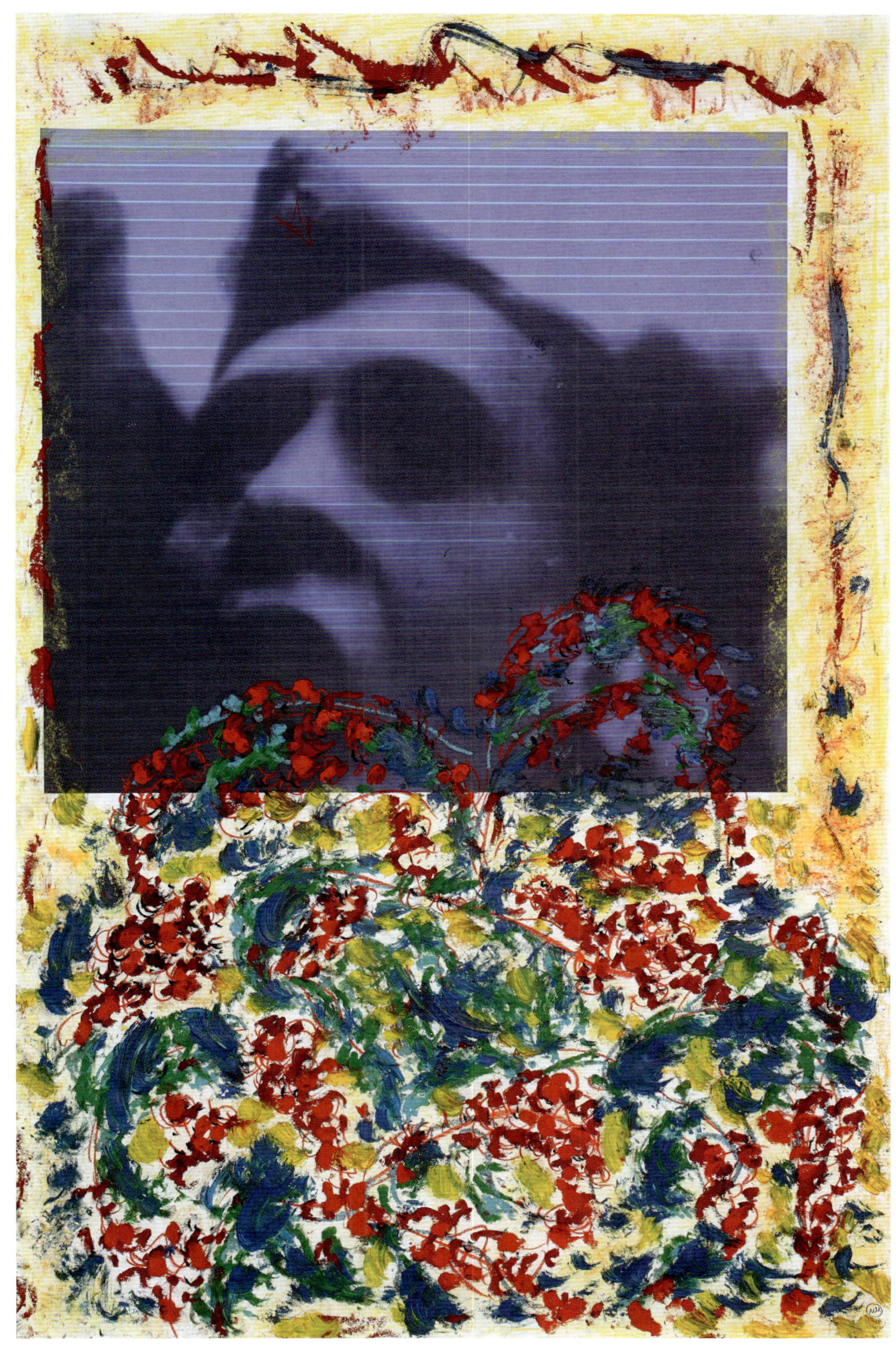

Last March 39, 2007
Digital print, oil sticks on paper,
36 x 24 in. / 91.44 x 60.96 cm

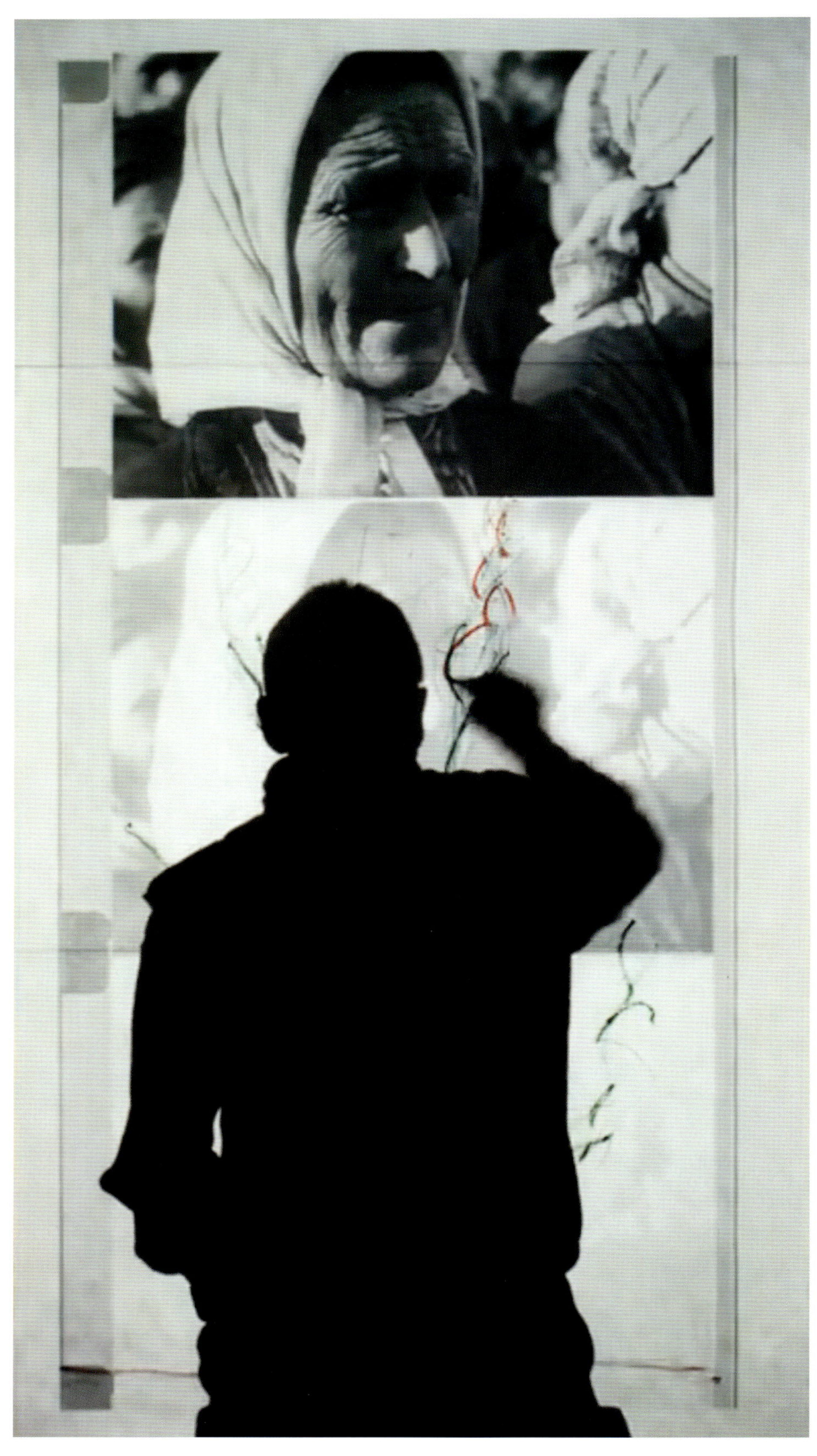

Trevor Tweeten and Naum Medovoy, *The Missing
(The Last March)*, 2014, still (detail)

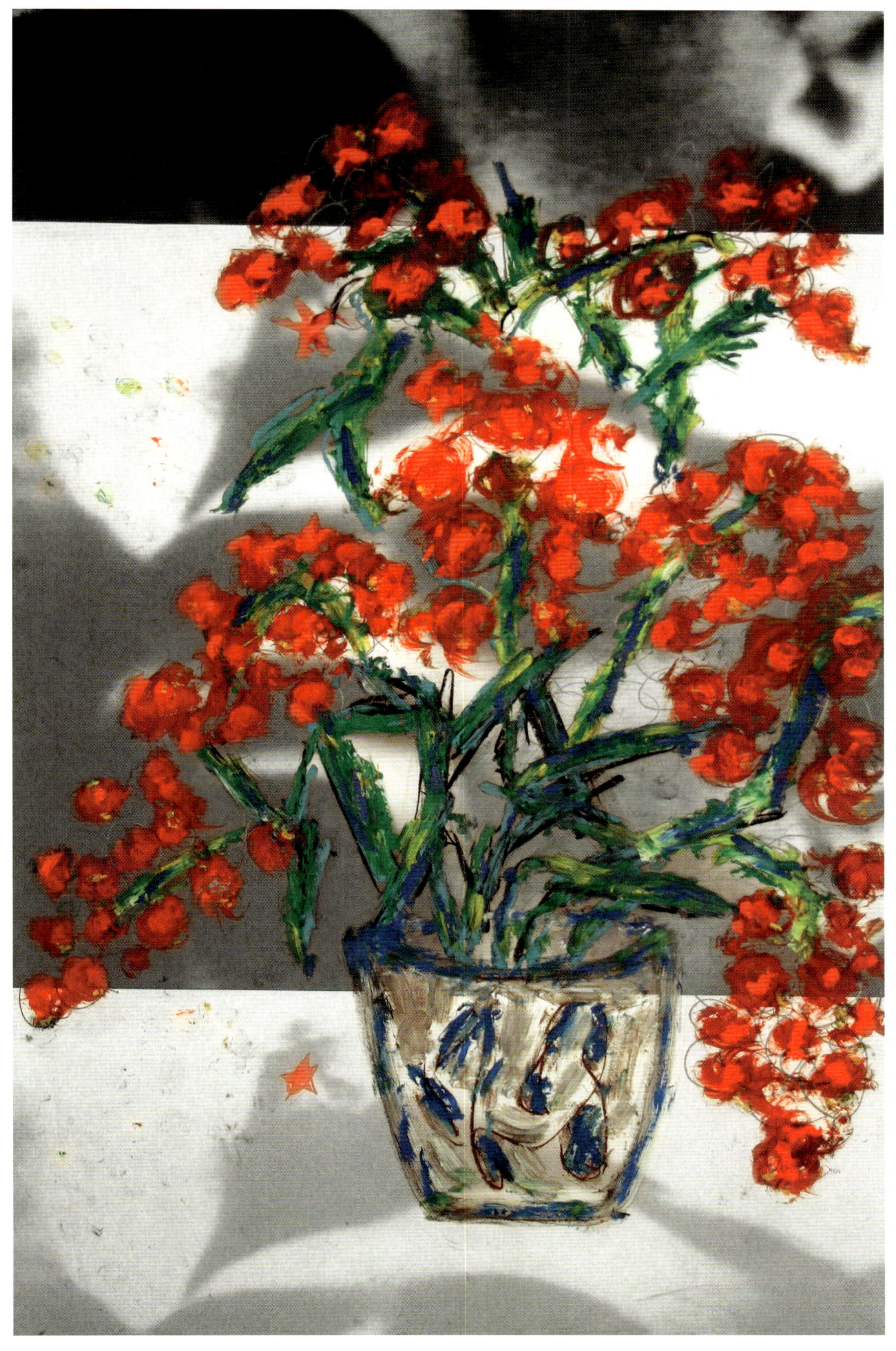

Last March 14, 2007
Digital print, oil sticks on paper,
42 x 24 in. / 106.68 x 60.96 cm

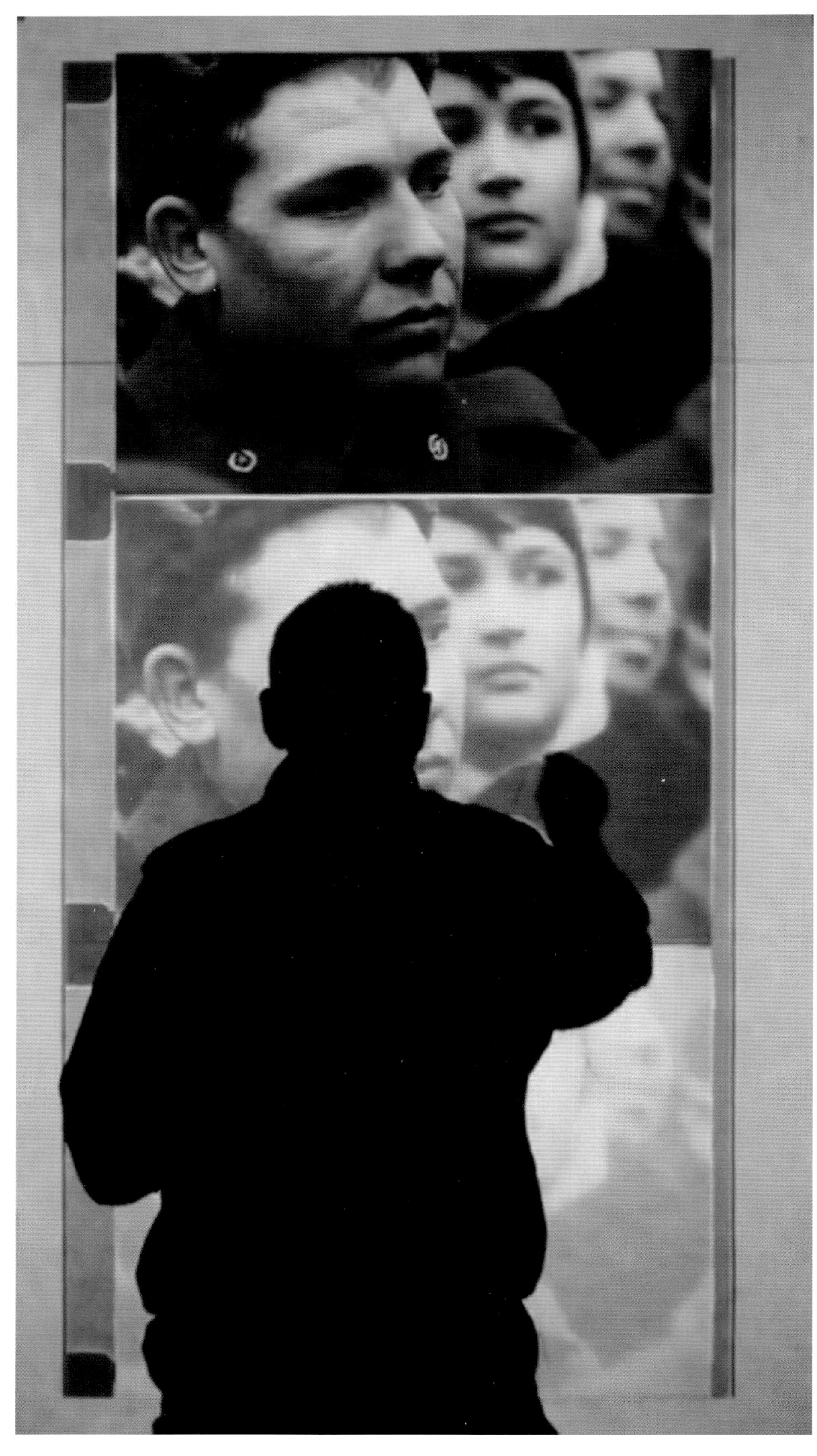

Trevor Tweeten and Naum Medovoy, *The Missing
(The Last March)*, 2014, still (detail)

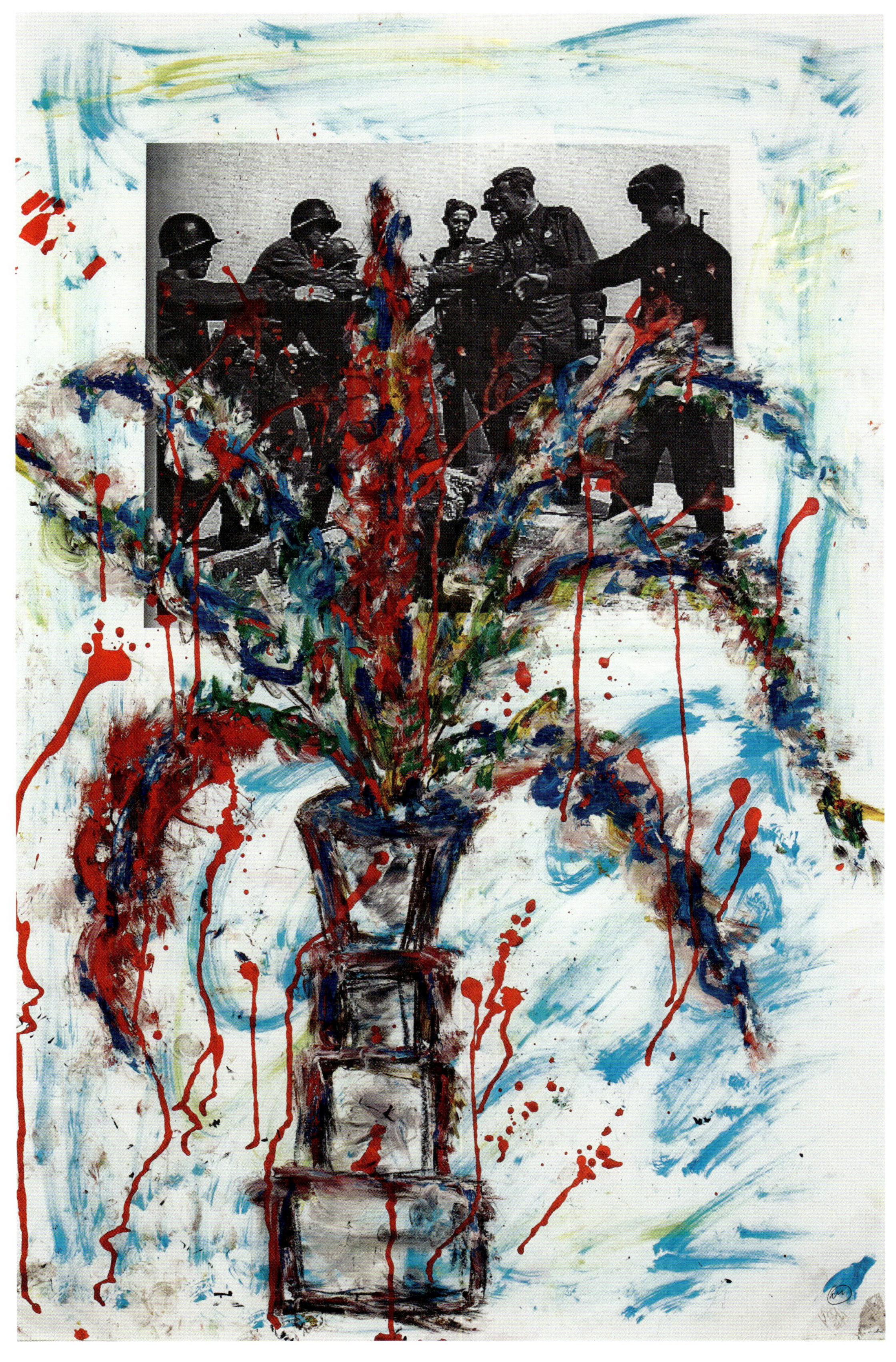

Last March 41, 2007
Digital print, oil sticks on paper,
36 x 24 in. / 91.44 x 60.96 cm

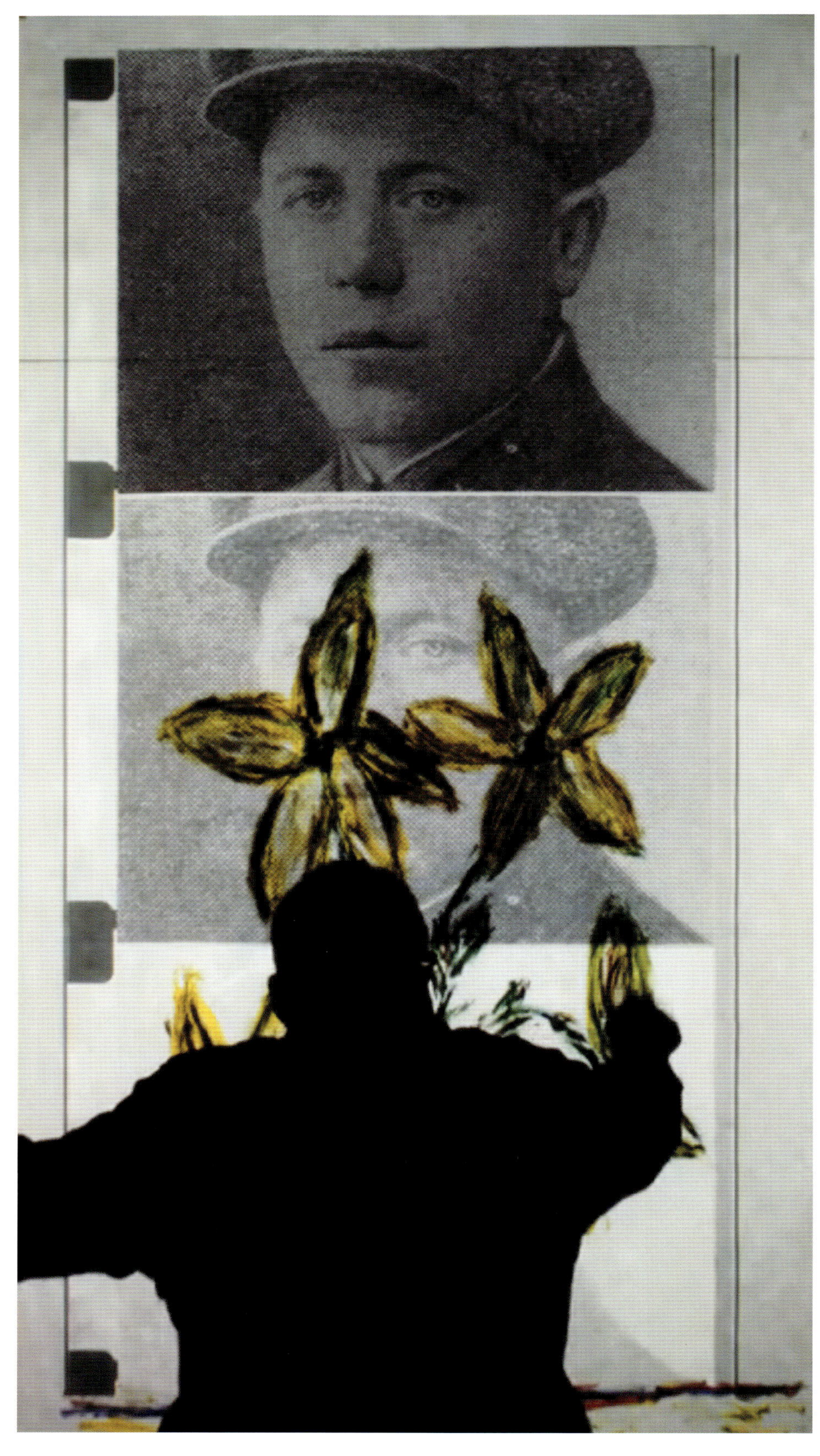

Trevor Tweeten and Naum Medovoy, *The Missing*
(*The Last March*), 2014, still (detail)

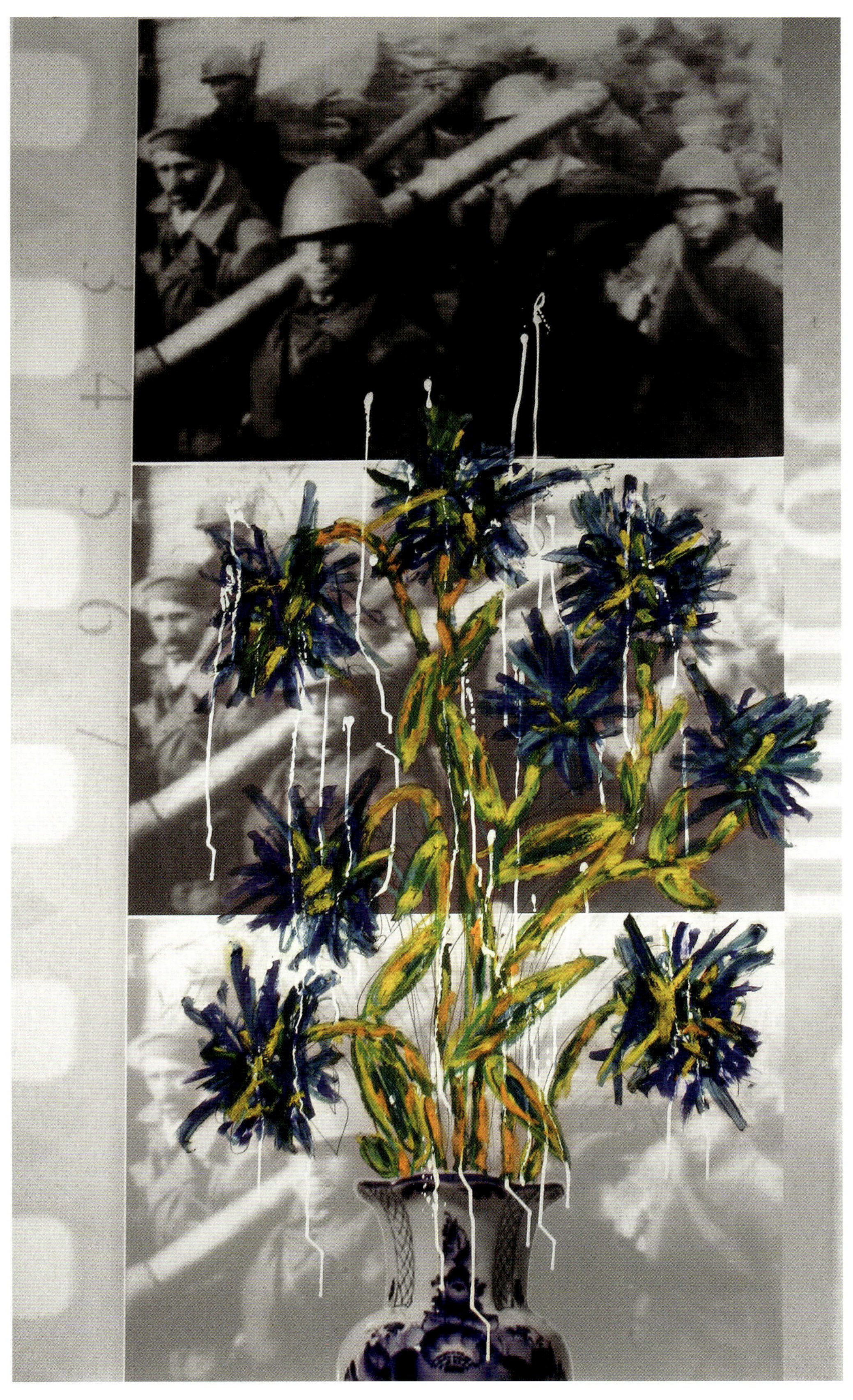

Last March 32, 2007
Digital print, oil sticks on paper,
66 ½ x 39 in. / 168.91 x 99.06 cm

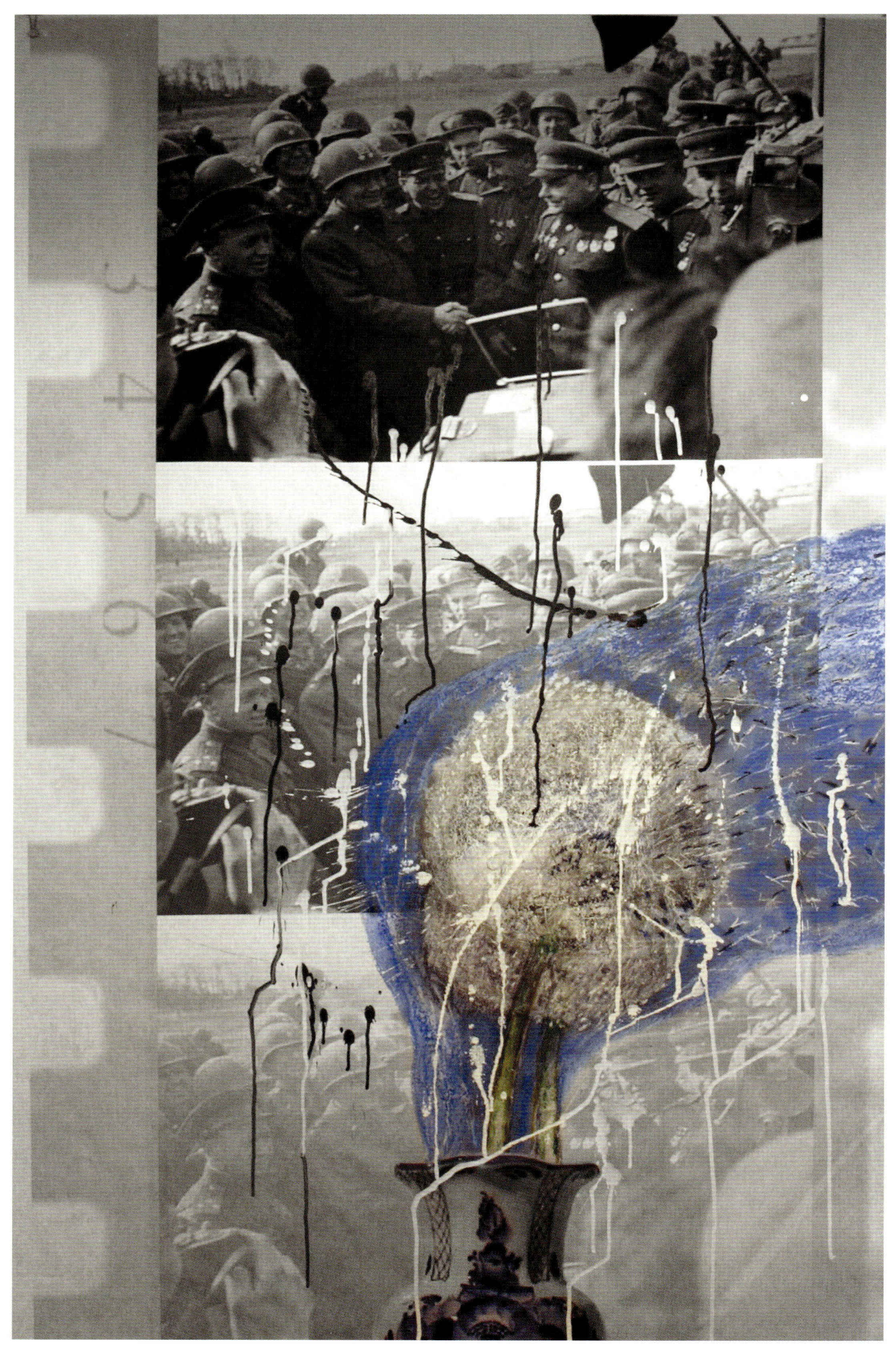

Last March 22, 2007
Digital print, oil sticks on paper,
42 x 24 in. / 106.68 x 60.96 cm

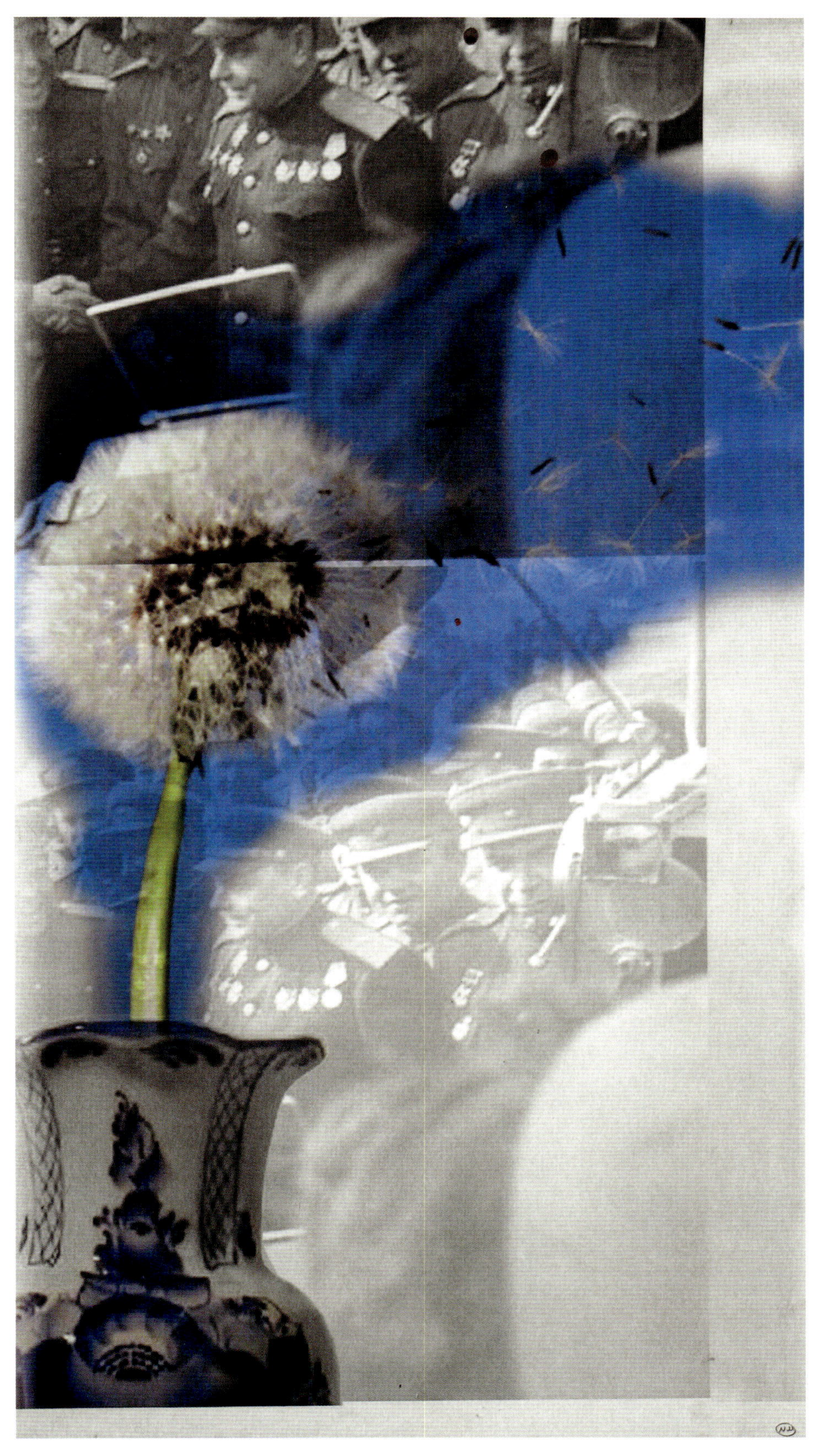

Last March 24, 2007
Digital print, oil sticks on paper,
67 x 39 in. / 170.18 x 99.06 cm

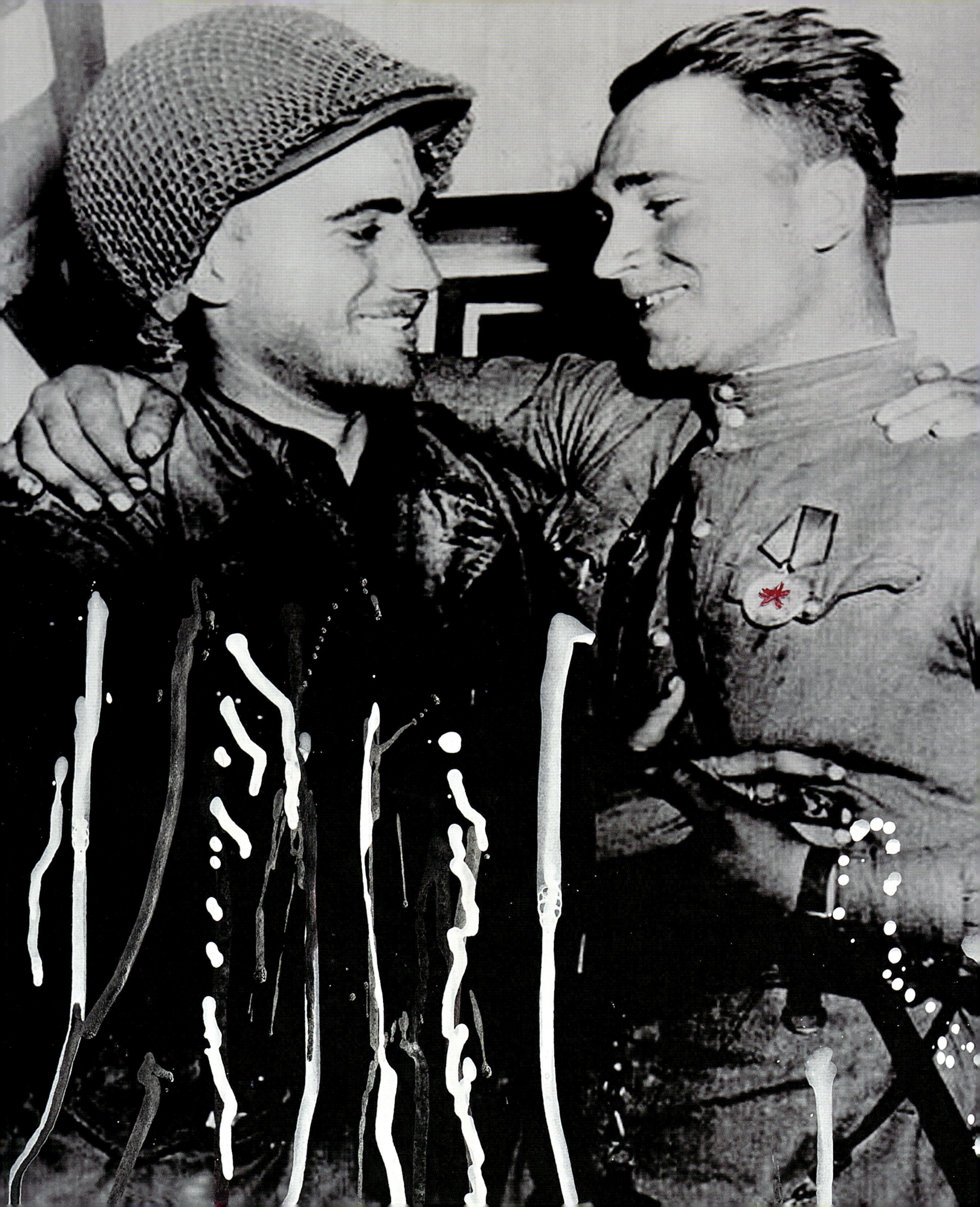

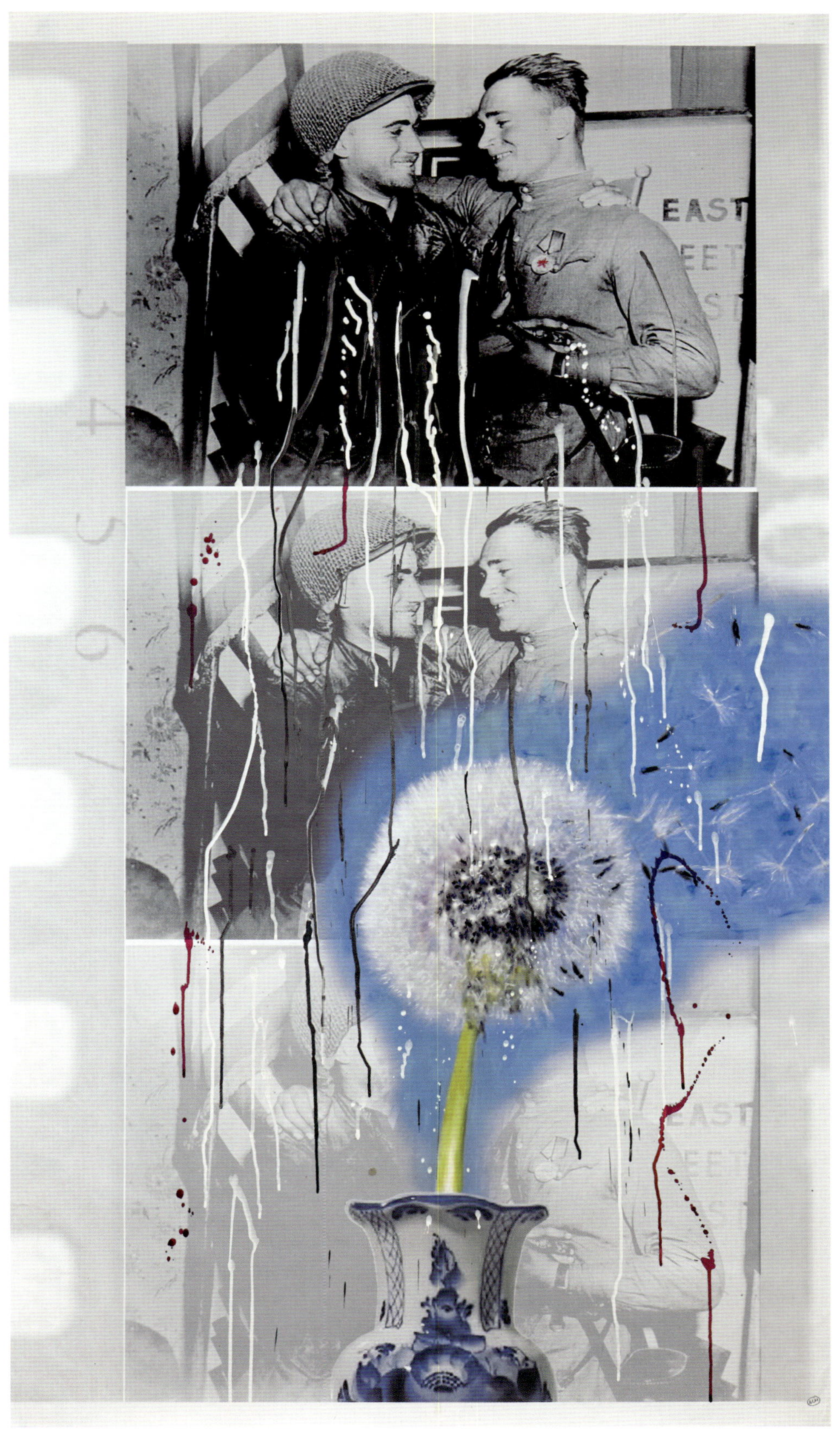

pp. 62, 64–65
Last March 23, 2007 (details)

Last March 23, 2007
Digital print, oil sticks on paper,
66 ½ x 39 in. / 168.91 x 99.06 cm

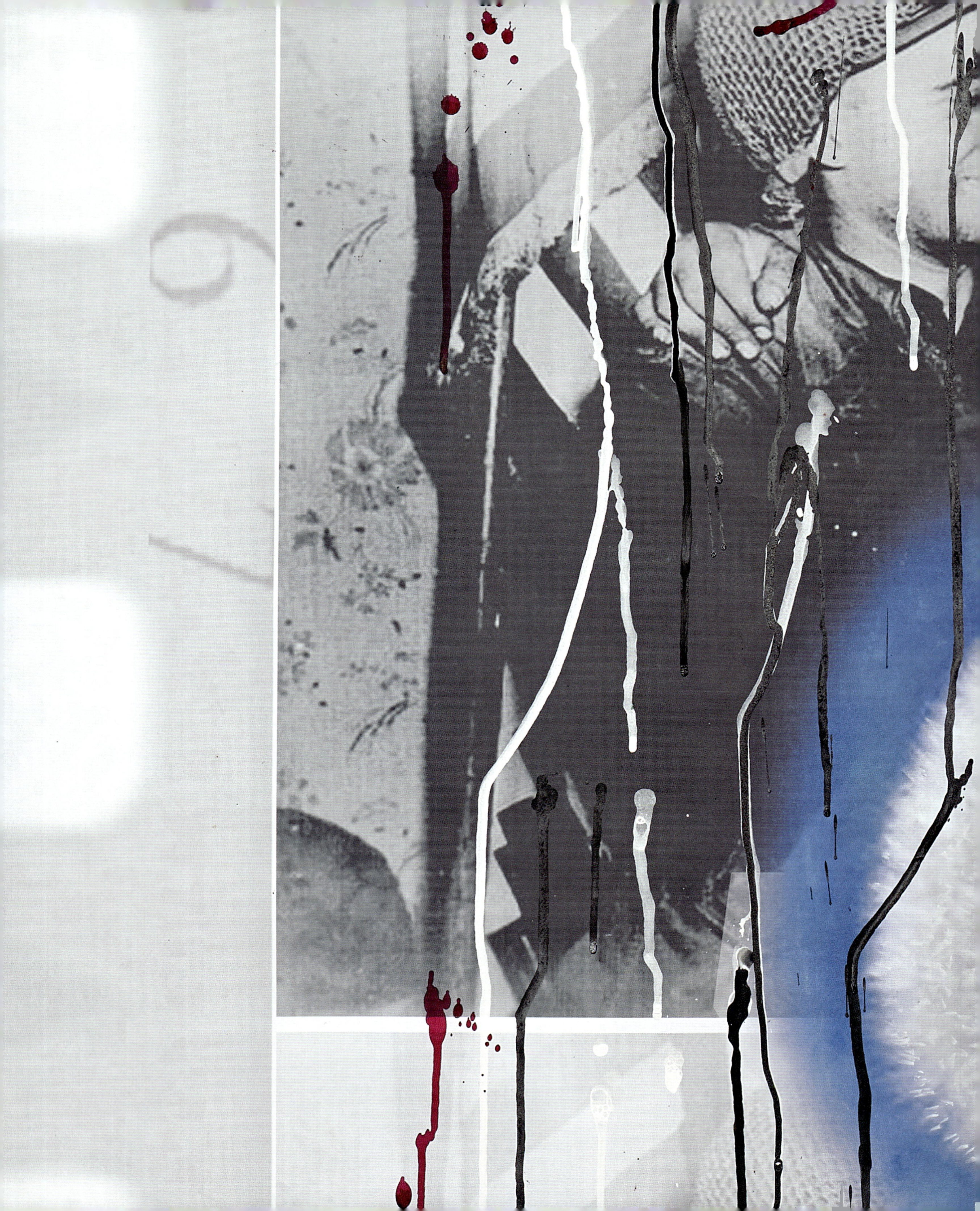

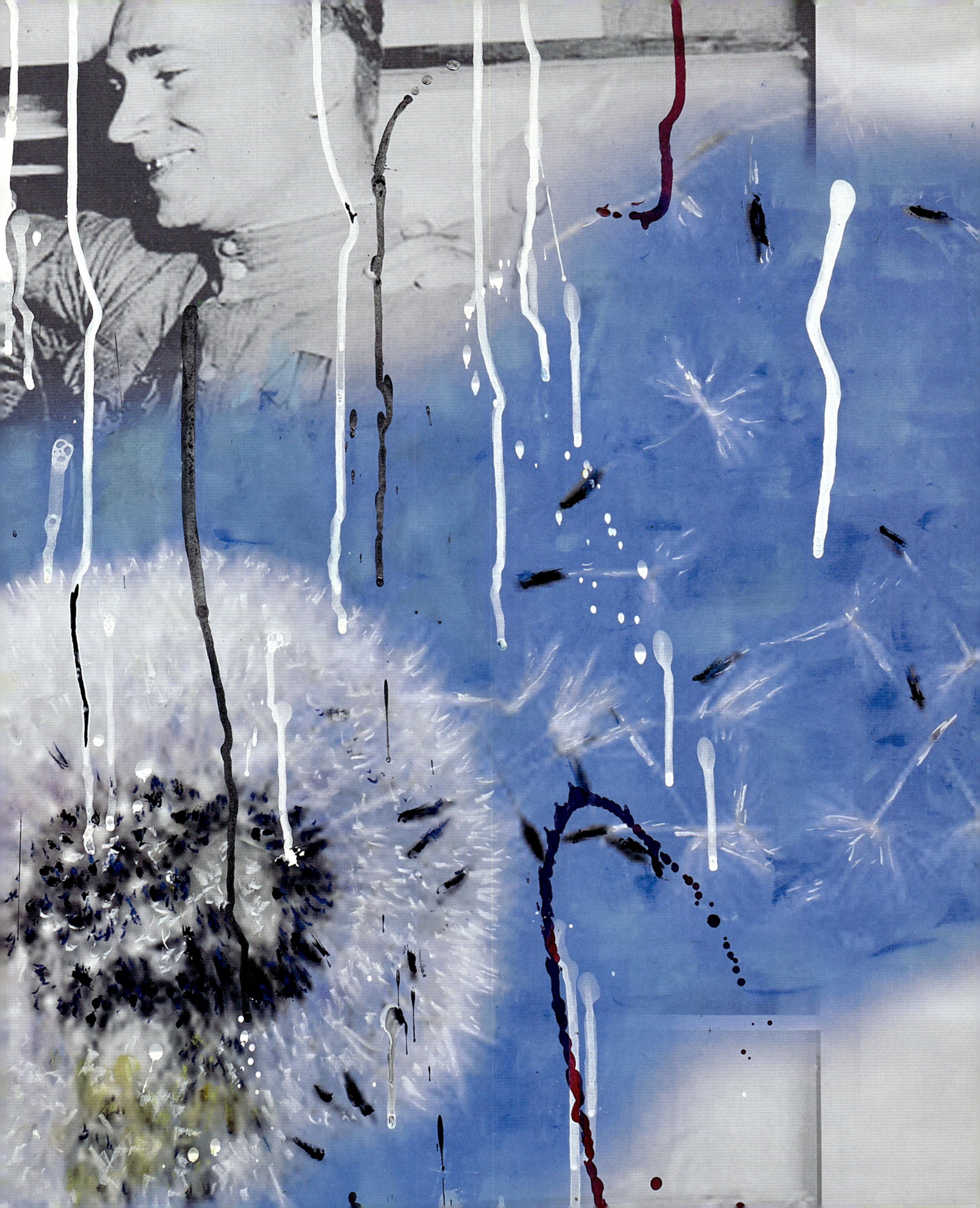

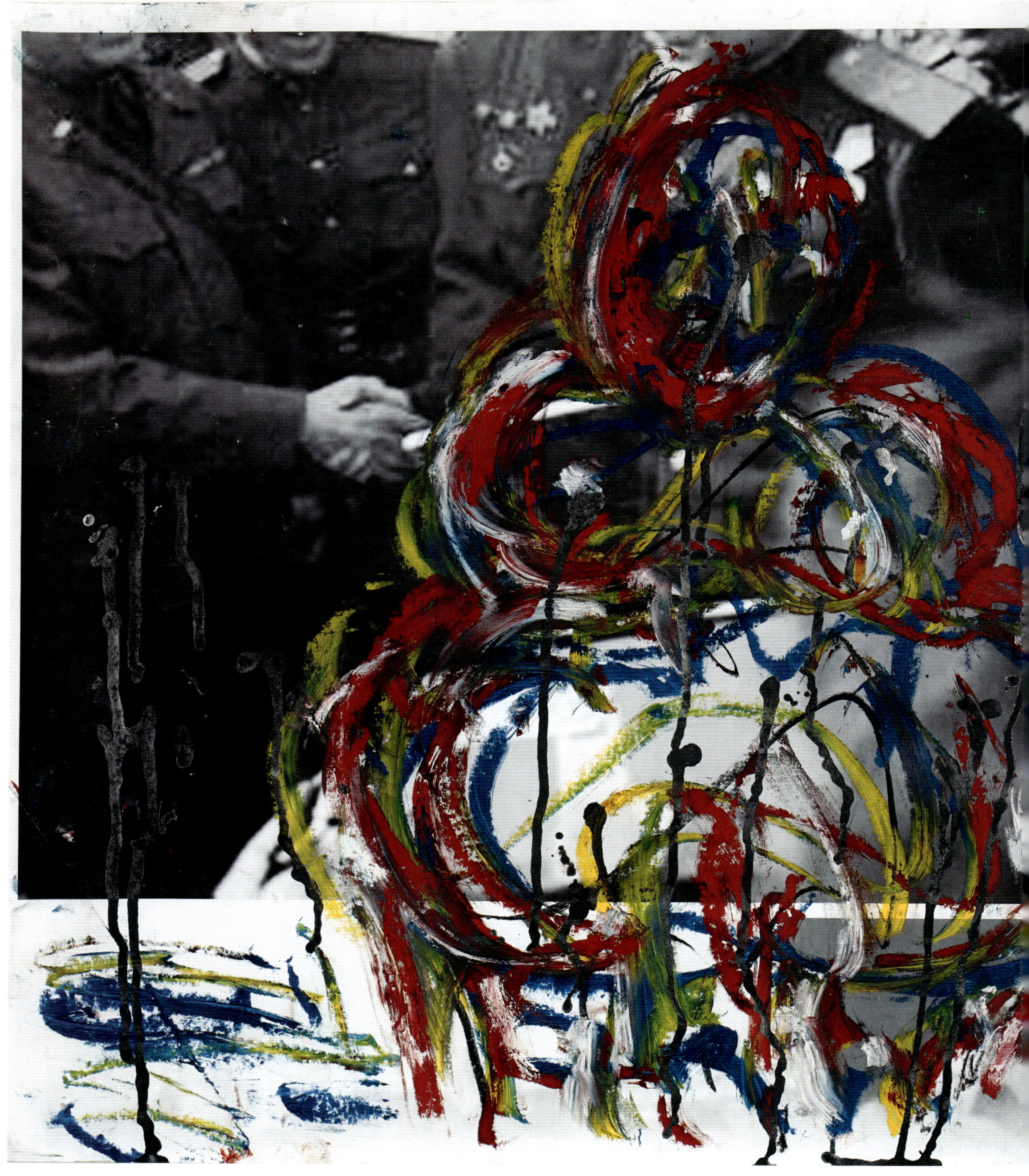

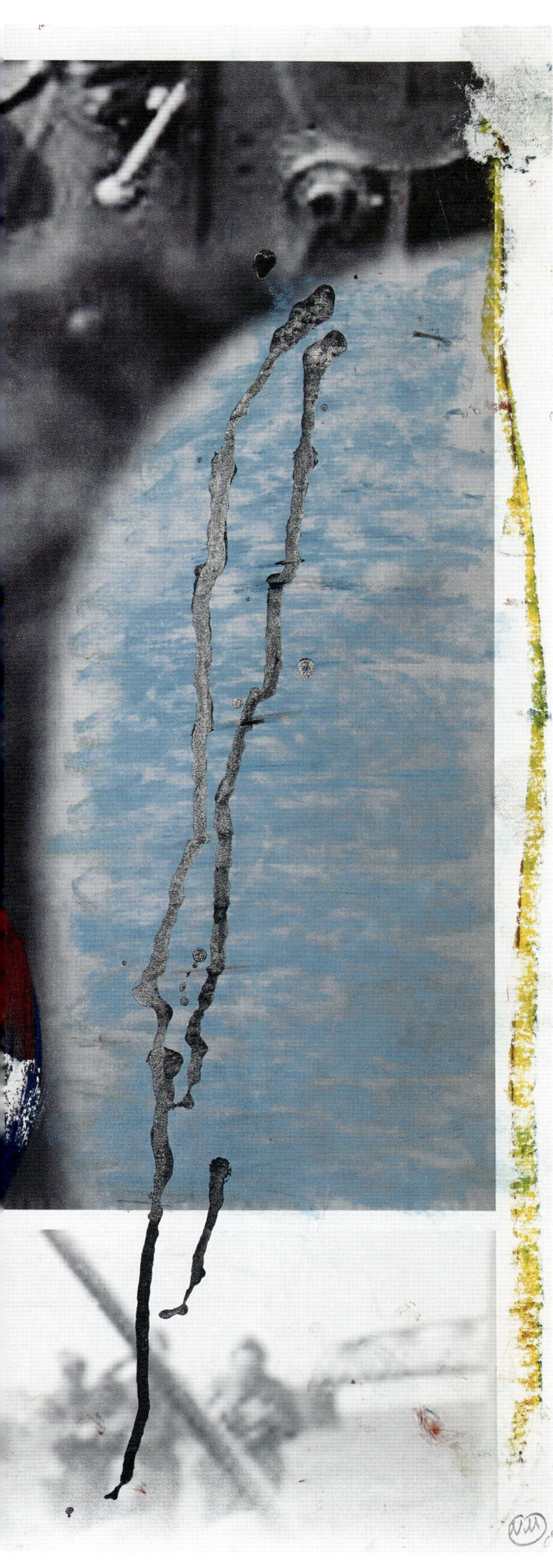

Last March 2, 2007
Digital print, oil sticks on paper,
18 ½ x 25 in. / 46.99 x 63.50 cm

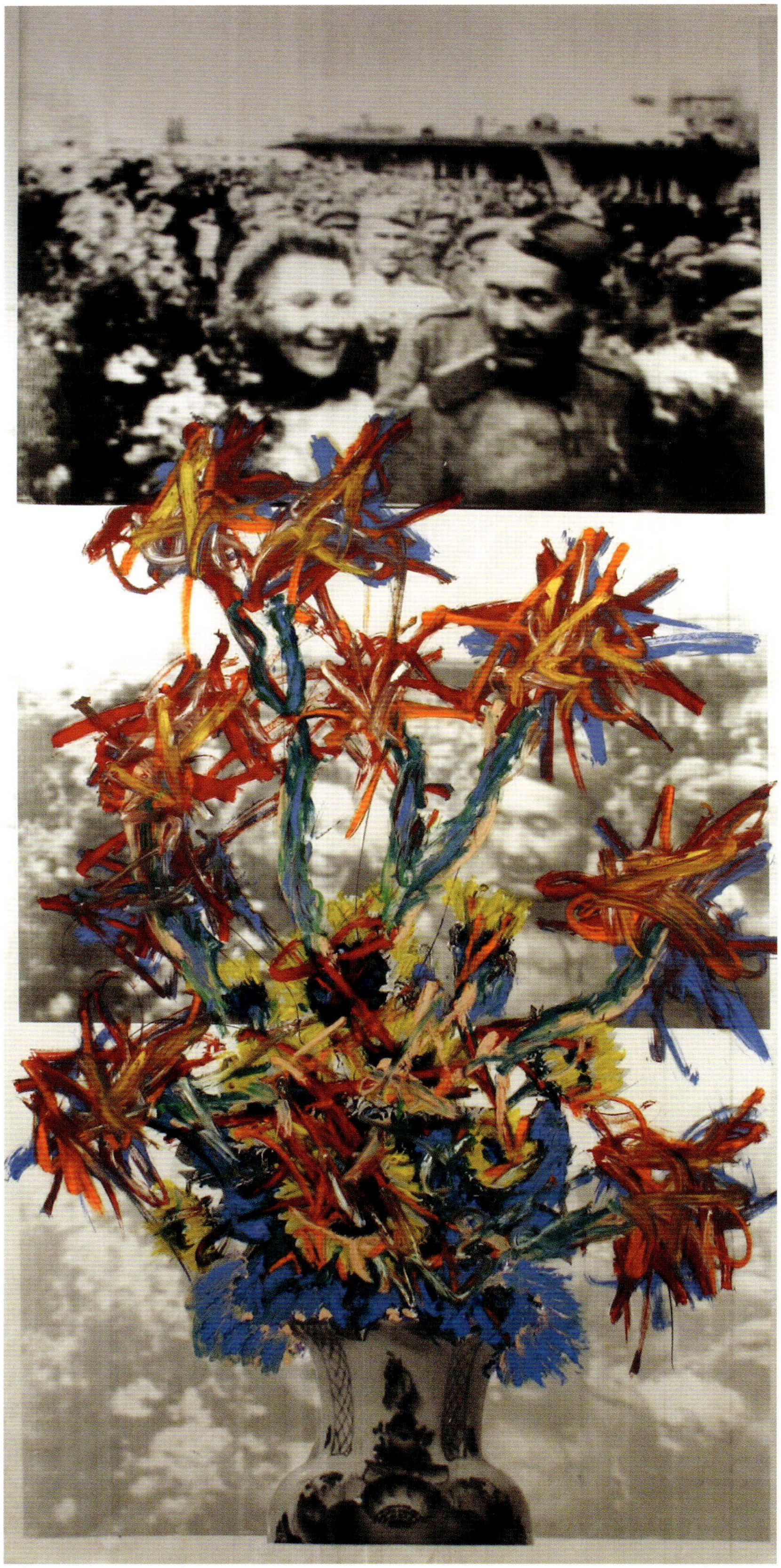

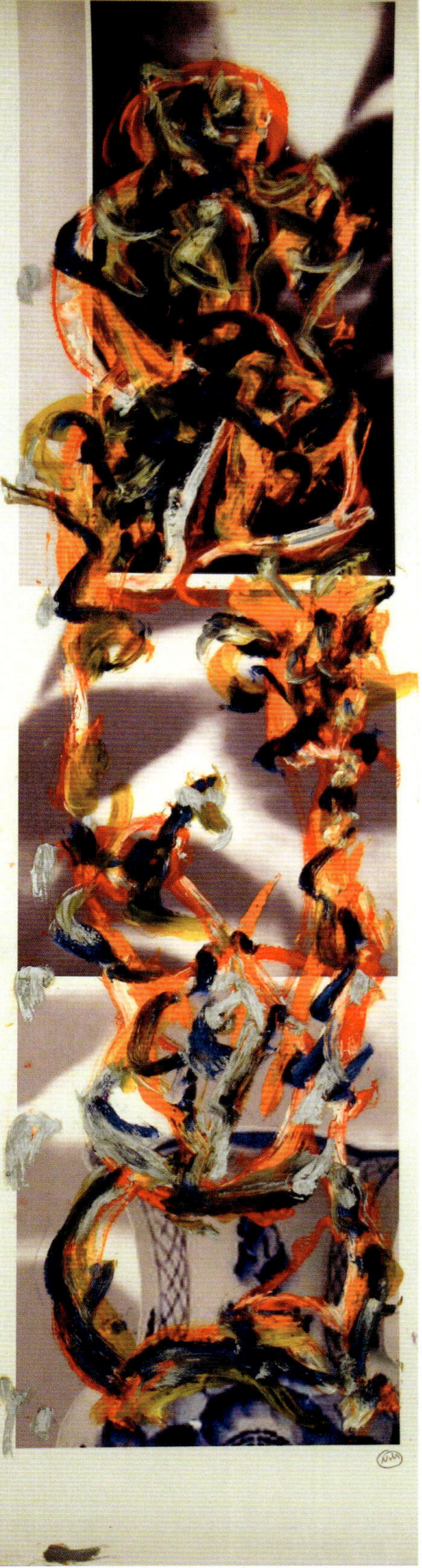

Last March 18, 2007
Digital print, oil sticks on paper,
76 ½ x 36 in. / 194.31 x 60.96 cm

Last March 34, 2007
Digital print, oil sticks on paper,
44 x 11 in. / 111.76 x 27.94 cm

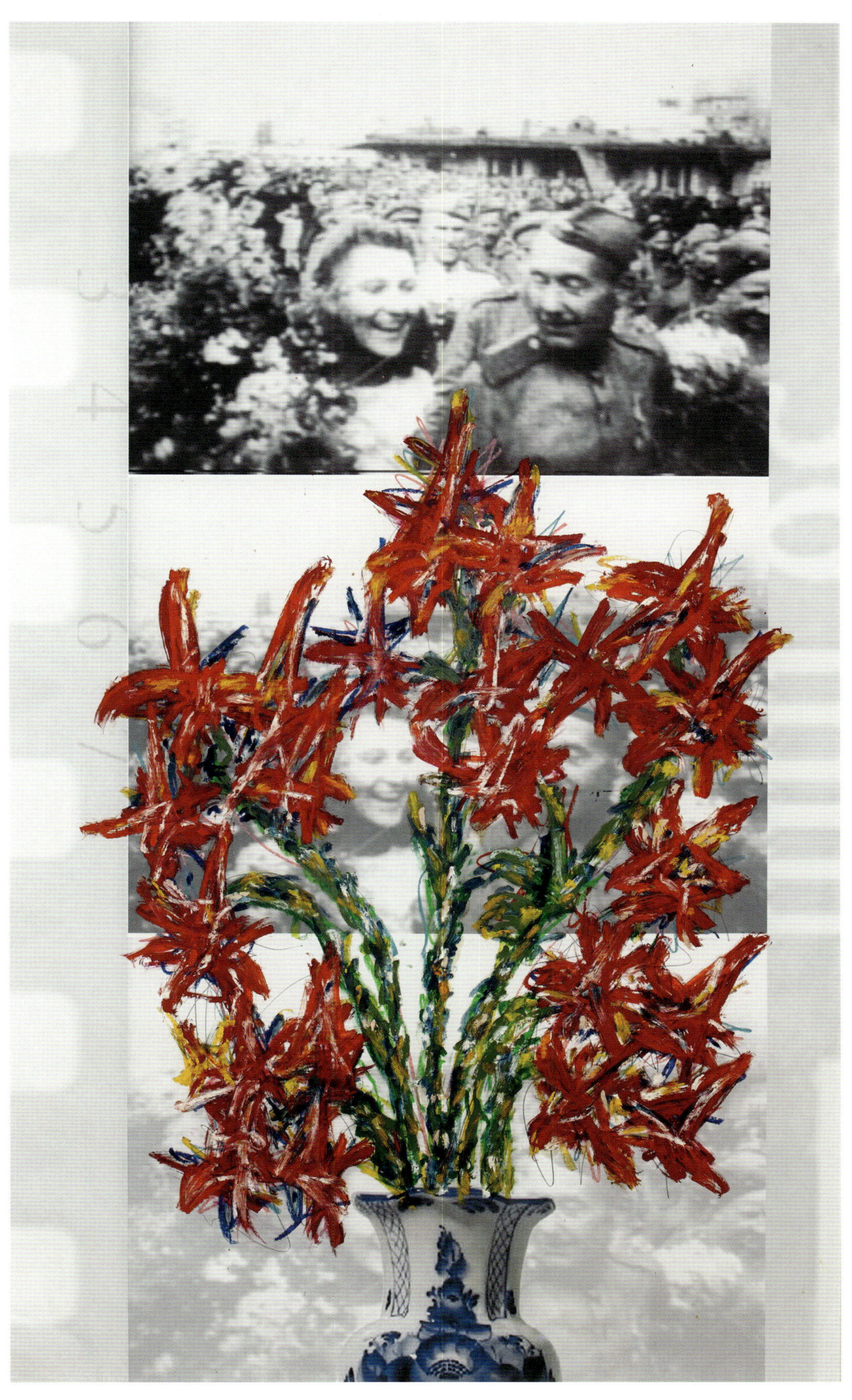

Last March 4, 2007
Digital print, oil sticks on paper,
24 x 18 in. / 60.96 x 45.72 cm

pp. 70–71
Last March 4, 2007 (detail)

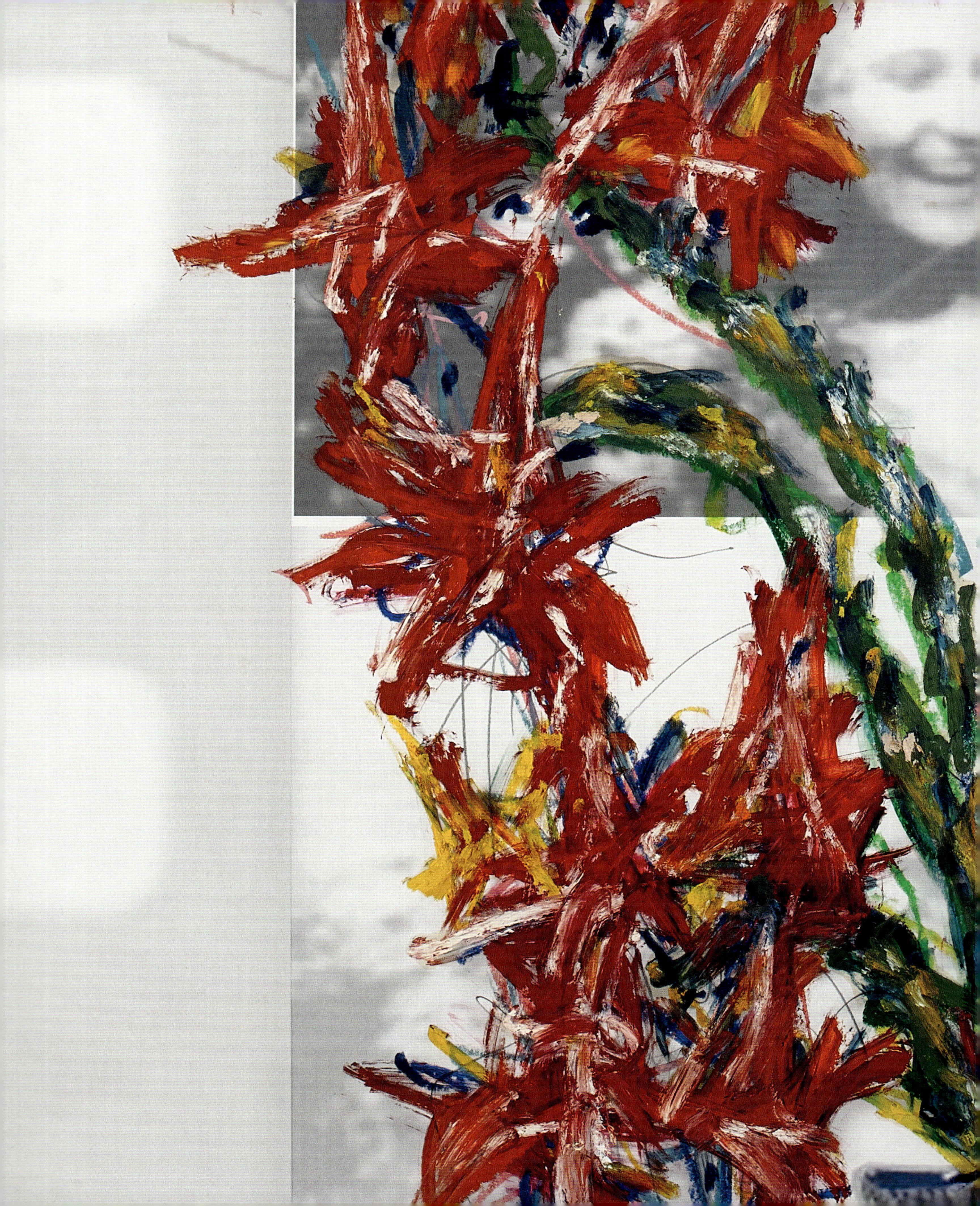

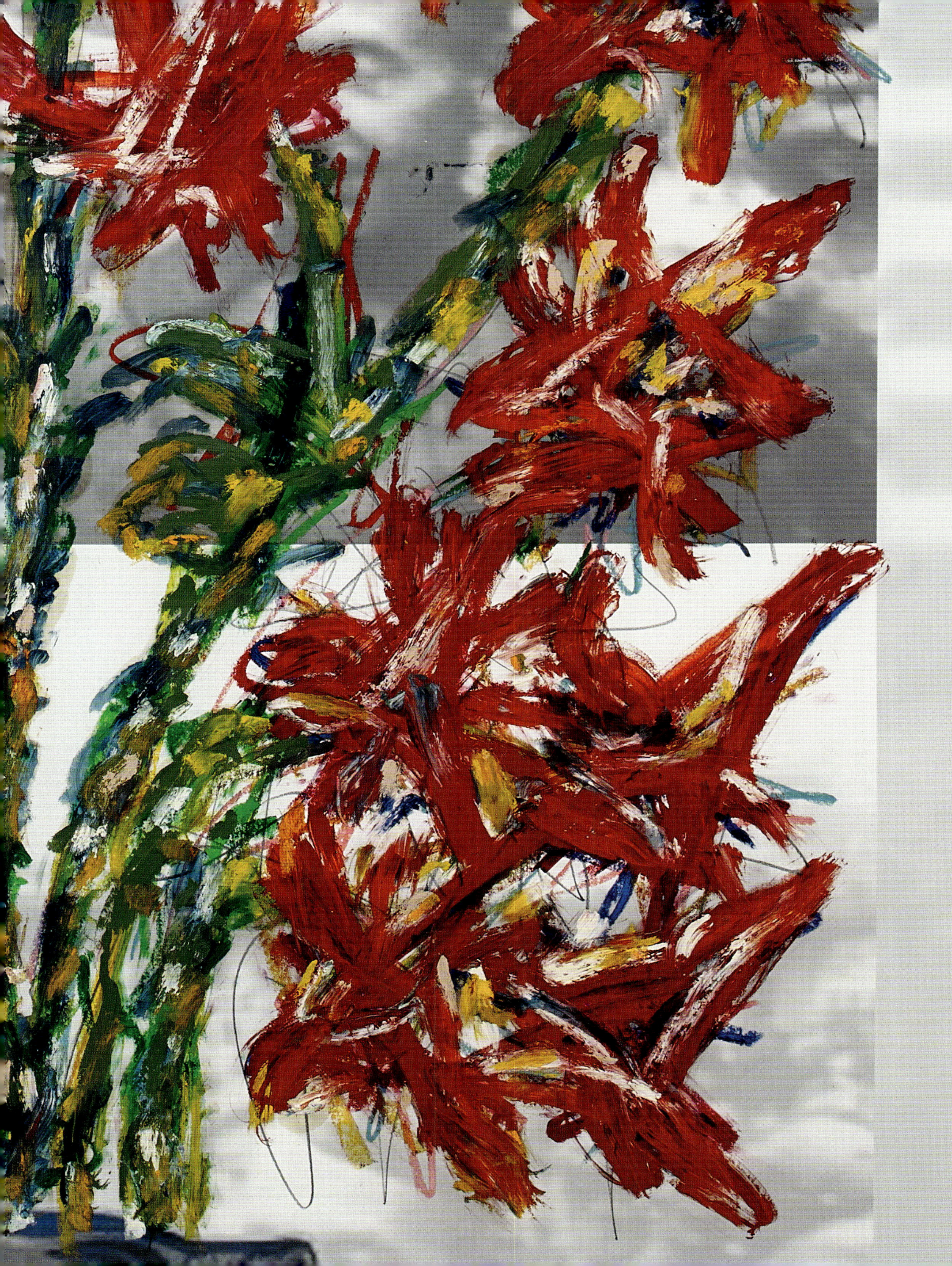

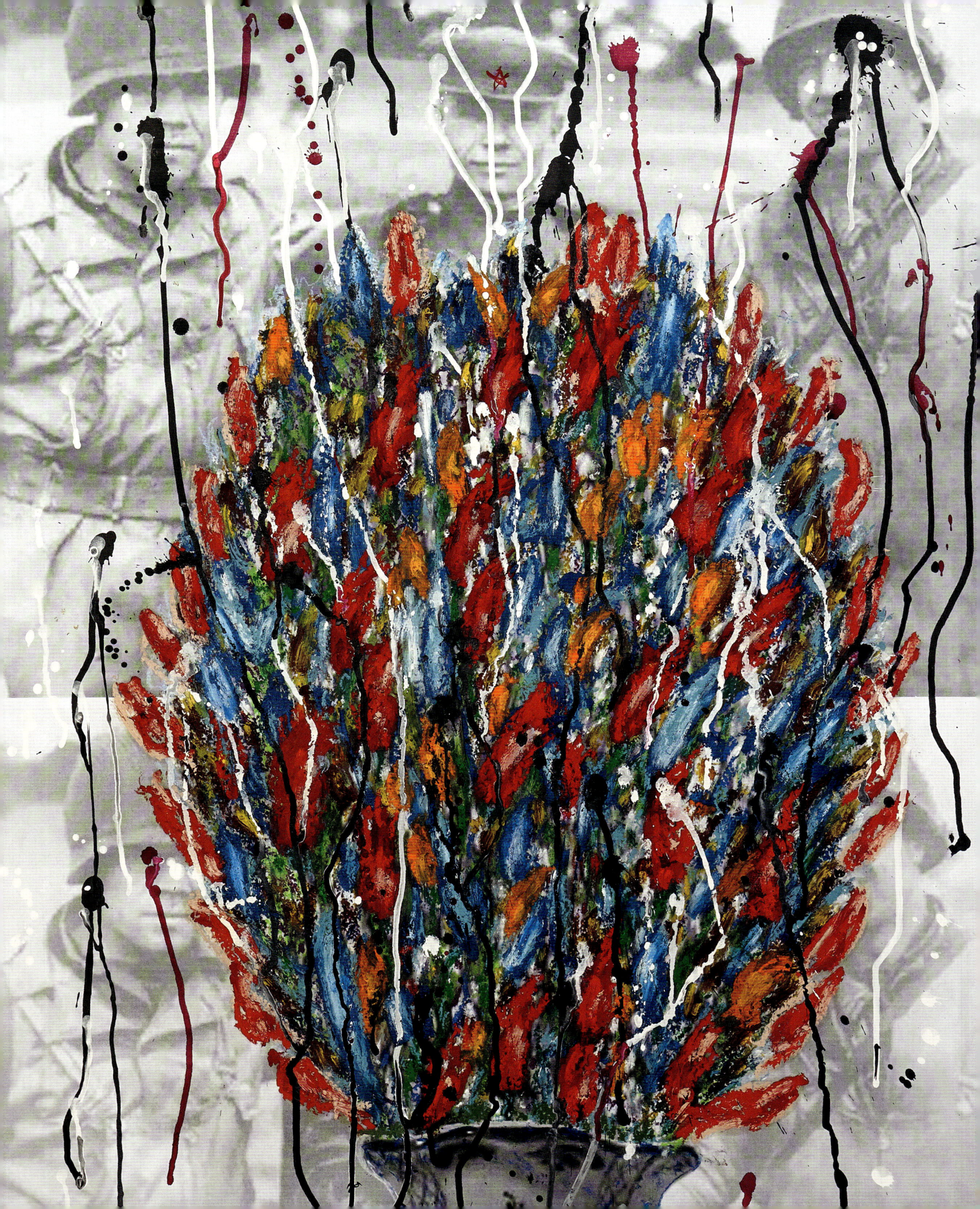

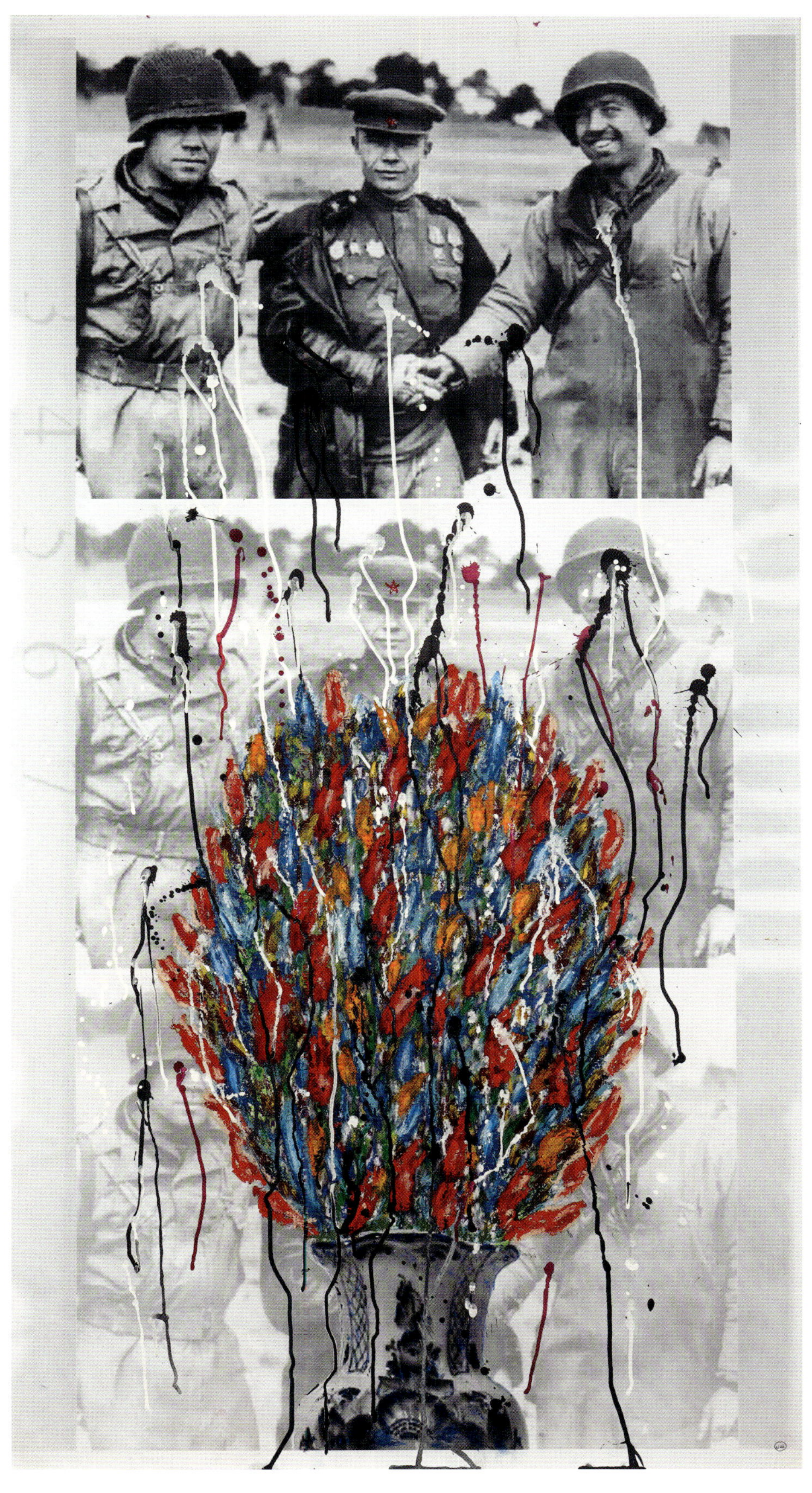

Last March 20, 2007 (detail)

Last March 20, 2007
Digital print, oil sticks on paper,
65 x 36 in. / 165.1 x 60.96 cm

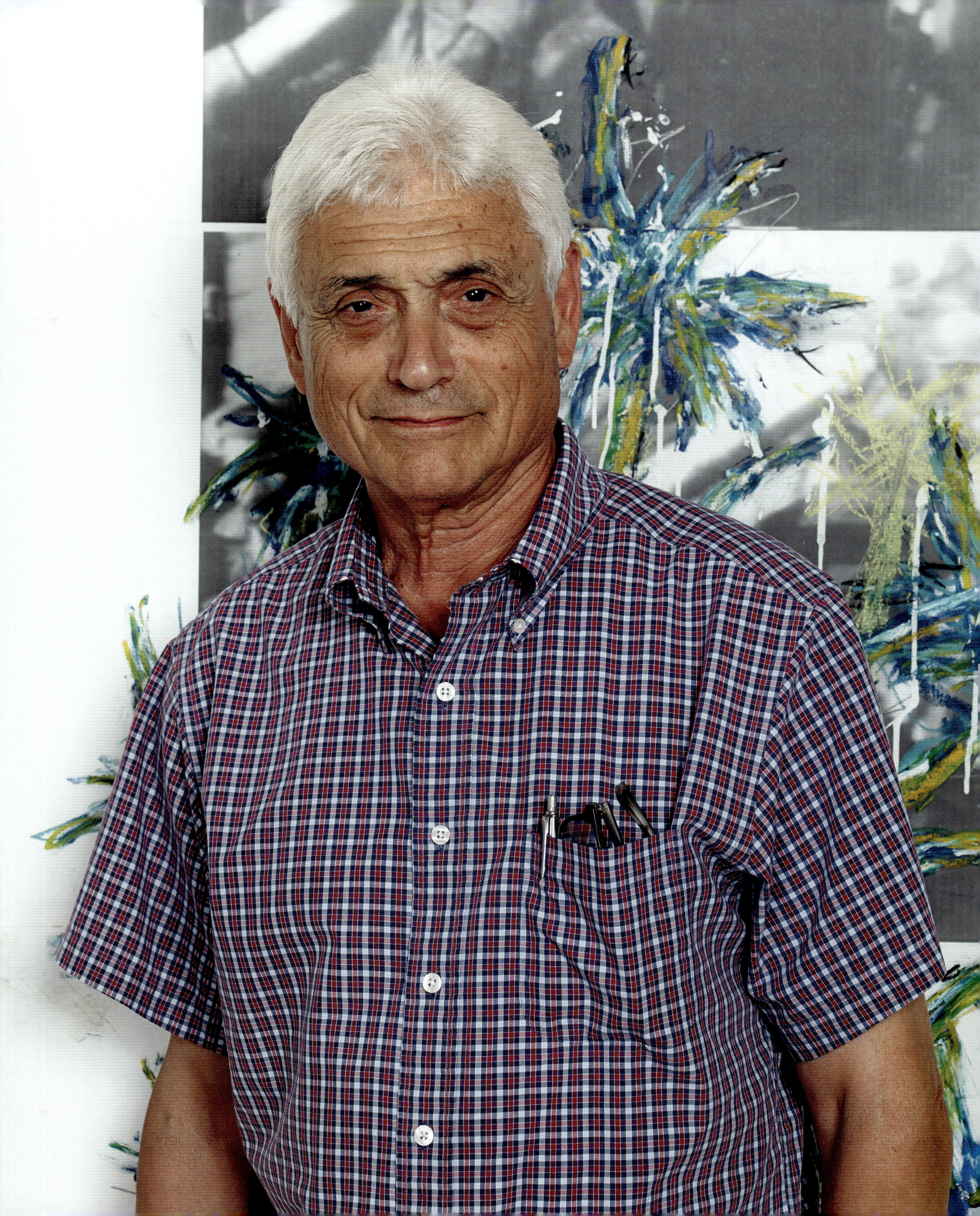

Biography

Born in Odessa, 1937

Education
1980–1982 New York University, NY
1962–1964 Film School, Moscow
1954–1959 Polytechnic Institute, Odessa

Solo Exhibitions
Salamatina Gallery, New York, 2013
Salamatina Gallery, New York, 2012
Museum of Russian Art, Jersey City NJ, 2011

Selected Group Exhibitions
Salamatina Gallery, New York, 2012
Salamatina Gallery, New York, 2011
Salamatina Gallery, New York, 2010
The National Arts Club, New York, 2009
The National Arts Club, New York, 2007

Other Projects
The Tretyakov Gallery, Moscow, "Night of Museums - 2012," an exhibition project called *Triumph Kaissa. Dedication to Marcel Duchamp*, organized in the framework of the cultural program of the World Chess Championship, May 2012
Elem Klimov, *Rasputin/"Agoniya"* (original title), 1981
The Last March, in collaboration with Jim Khlevner (documentary), 1972
Elem Klimov, *Sport, sport, sport* (documentary), 1970

Public Collections
Multimedia Art Museum, Moscow
Jewish Museum and Tolerance Center, Moscow
Museum of the Great Patriotic War, Moscow
The Chess Museum, Moscow

Catalogue Texts for Solo Exhibitions
"Naum Medovoy," John Cauman, 2013
"Naum Medovoy," Oksana Salamatina, 2013
"Naum Medovoy and His Art," John William Narins, 2011

Catalogue Texts for Group Exhibitions
"A Little Game Between 'I' and 'Me': Marcel Duchamp, Chess, and New York Dada," Bradley Bailey, 2012

Video Documentation of Solo Exhibitions
On Russian Contemporary Art, Salamatina Gallery and Hugo Perez, 2014
Naum Medovoy: A Portrait of an Artist, Salamatina Gallery and Hugo Perez, 2013

Selected Articles in Books, Publications, Newspapers and Digital
"Naum Medovoy: Last March," *Blouin Artinfo* (digital), May 2013
"Naum Medovoy: Last March." *Itar - Tass* (digital), May 23, 2013
"Naum Medovoy: Last March." *Itar - Tass* (digital), May 18, 2013

Naum Medovoy in his studio
in New York City, 2014
© photo Max Yawney

Oksana Salamatina / Salamatina Gallery

Oksana Salamatina is the founder and owner of Salamatina Gallery (Manhasset, New York), which represents both established and emerging contemporary artists. The gallery's exhibitions have been featured *The New York Times*, *The New Yorker*, *Art News* and *Sculpture Magazine*, amongst other publications, and the gallery's artists have been exhibited at the New Museum (New York), the National Portrait Gallery (Washington DC), the Smithsonian Art Museum (Washington DC), the Centre Georges Pompidou (Paris, France), the Tretyakov State Gallery (Moscow, Russia), SF MoMA (San Francisco), and the Bass Museum of Art (Miami), as well as in numerous other institutions and galleries.

Before opening Salamatina Gallery in 2008, Oksana worked at both the New Museum and at the Nassau County Museum of Art, where she collaborated on a number of important exhibitions. Prior to her museum experience, Oksana worked for both Sotheby's and Christie's. She holds two Master's degrees: one in International Economics from the State University of Commerce, Moscow, and another in Art Gallery Administration from FIT (Fashion Institute of Technology), State University of New York. She was also the recipient of a Guggenheim Scholarship in 1998 and spent that summer at the Peggy Guggenheim Collection, Venice.

Contributors

Rahim Azimov, Anastasia Barysheva, John Cauman, David Everitt Howe, Elena Filatova, Amanda Glesmann, Paola Gribaudo, Simon Hewitt, Nic Iljine, Vasily Klyukin, Vitaly Komar, Alexa Makhina, Marina Mayorova, Michael Medovoy, Daniel Neumann, Susanna Neumann, Hugo Perez, David Rager, Alexander Robins, Anatoli Salamatin, Tatiana Salamatina, Andrea Traubner, Trevor Tweeten, Max Yawney